WORKING MUSICIAN

THE STORY OF JAMES WALSH AND GYPSY

BY AL ZDON AND JAMES WALSH

MOONLIT EAGLE PRODUCTIONS
MINNEAPOLIS, MINNESOTA

Published by
Moonlit Eagle Productions

For information, address: Moonlit Eagle Productions
5064 Irondale Road, Mounds View, MN 55112

ISBN: 978-0-9711940-5-2

Manufactured in the United States of America

2025

To all the great bands of the 60s and 70s who led us where we've never been, and left us gasping.

ACKNOWLEDGEMENTS

In the end, a book is created with dozens, maybe hundreds of people contributing. We would like to acknowledge every person who is named in this book. Special thanks go to those who did lengthy interviews including Rick Ballot, Doni Larson, Jay Epstein and Bill Davis.

The cover art was commissioned by Rick Reed and drawn by Bruce Peterson. It was a cherished piece of art for James Walsh, and he requested that it be used on the cover.

Thanks to minniepaulmusic.com, a premiere website devoted to the music of the 1955 to 1975 era in the Twin Cities, and to Denny Johnson for his permission to use pictures from the site. Anybody who has an interest in Minnesota rock and roll from those times should visit the website.

In addition to MinniePaul, pictures came from many people, and we have tried to identify the source for every picture.

Thanks to Jan Rangel for her help in finding pictures and for her depth of knowledge about Gypsy.

Thanks to Dennis Donovan, Mary Zdon, Darold "Deb" Wold and Sandy Peterson for proofreading. Any mistakes left in the book are James' and mine. Special thanks to Dennis for coming forward with his support at a crucial time. And ultra special thanks to my friends Connie Vincent and Greg "Boomer" Moritko, without whom you wouldn't be holding this book.

Thanks to Isaac Huss for creating the Working Musican website. Liina Lundin, one of the Twin Cities' best graphic designers, created the book cover.

We acknowledge the spiritual forces in our lives that keep us on the straight and narrow, and gave us the strength to complete this book.

NOTE ON THE BOOK'S STRUCTURE

The book is mainly an autobiography of James Walsh. The heart of the book is James Walsh telling his story. When you start a chapter, that's Jim's voice. Built around these chapters are essays, done by Al Zdon, sidebars, interviews and other material aimed at providing some additional information about Walsh and Gypsy and the times. It's a little eclectic. The best way to describe it is Progressive Rock Journalism.

One more note on the use of "Owl" as a nickname for James Walsh. It is used rarely in the book, and some may wonder why. Jim said the sobriquet was created by friends because he was often up late at night reading, and it wasn't because he looked like a wise, old owl. In any case, he eschewed the nickname later in life, and when it was suggested that "Owl" could be the name of the book, he quickly quashed that idea.

The Underbeats carried on when Jim Johnson went in the Army and served in Vietnam. From left: Tom Nystrom, Enrico Rosenbaum, Doni Larson, Loren Walstad, James Walsh. (Photo courtesy of Doni Larson)

PREFACE

Edison High School in Northeast Minneapolis takes up a full block of this immigrant neighborhood, rising with all the charm and architectural beauty of an industrial warehouse.

In the 1965 school year, both Al Zdon and James Walsh were assigned to Mrs. Miller's homeroom. It was a home ec room, and so the students sat at tables thus facilitating early morning conversations. Probably most people in the school knew that Walsh was in the Coronados, probably the top rock and roll band to emerge from a Northeast garage to play at teen clubs and school dances. Even in those early days of rock, being in a band carried enormous allure and magic.

Jim Walsh was at my table and so we chit-chatted each morning before heading off to our classes for the day. The Beatles were all the rage, and every band in Minnesota and in the world I suppose was compelled to cover Beatles' songs. Jim said the Coronados didn't have much trouble learning the music — it wasn't rocket science — but sometimes the lyrics were a problem.

At that time in my life, I found that if I saved the $2.50 I got from my parents for riding the bus to school each week and took my bike instead, I could go downtown on Saturday and pick out a new album at Dayton's Seventh Floor, the marketplace for new music in the Twin Cities.

I would choose a Peter, Paul and Mary, or a Kingston Trio or a Brothers Four, or a British Invasion band like Gerry and the Pacemakers, but of course I always got the latest Beatles album. There was some street cred in having the latest by the World's Greatest Band.

So I mentioned to Jim that I had the newest Beatles album, perhaps *Rubber Soul*. And he said, "Can you get me the words?" And so I did. I would play part of a song, lift the arm on my record player, furiously write down the words, and then put the arm down again. And then move back to where I missed.

And so over time, I gave Jim the words to songs like "Drive My Car" and "Nowhere Man," or "In My Life." I actually can't remember what songs I transcribed.

Part of Mrs. Miller's Room 108 homeroom in 1965-66 at Edison High School. At top is Jim Walsh, and at left on the bottom is Al Zdon. At right is another classmate, Dan Berg, who was voted Most Likely to Succeed in the graduating class of 1966.

And then Jim ran away and joined the circus — I mean he left the halls of Edison to become a full-time working musician, leaving school and our burgeoning relationship behind.

Flash forward 57 years, and I was convinced by some friends that we should go to a venue on Central Avenue to hear Gypsy, where Jim was still playing with the band. Before the show, we found Jim relaxing outside the tent. When I had a chance, I reminded him of the time I got lyrics for him in Mrs. Miller's homeroom. He had no memory of that. After a time, he went in the tent and Gypsy played and knocked my socks off. They still had it.

In the following weeks I ruminated about our long, interrupted relationship, and the wonderful way things twisted and turned to bring us together again. I had written several biographies, and the thought of a book crossed my mind. But, honestly, I wondered if I wanted to spend that much time with someone I'm not sure I really liked in high school.

But Jim's long trek through the music industry — and the allure of Gypsy — made me want to write the story. Gypsy never made the charts in any significant way, but they were the best band to come out of Minnesota in that era. They were the house band at the premier West Coast rock and roll bar, Whisky a Go Go, for two years, and they played nearly every major and minor venue in the United States, including the Atlanta Pop Festival, one of the largest gatherings of humanity in the planet's history.

So I finally sent an email, and outlined my bona fides such as having written other books. The e-note got as far as Jan Rangel, who was monitoring Jim's email account (Jim did about as much electronic communication as he needed), and she relayed it to Jim. She replied and said that Jim was interested.

It's been a good journey. It's fun to put two classmates together again so many years later, like bringing fraternal twins together after 50 plus years. We can talk to each other just like we hadn't skipped a beat because we have a common language. You can take the boy out of Northeast but you can't take the Northeast out of the boy. We can crack each other up, laugh a lot, and share insights. I learned a lot of how to talk "musician," and that's an interesting adventure in itself.

So here's the book. I think it's worthwhile. I think it's one of the better looks at the Minneapolis music scene of the late 60s, particularly the down-home accounts by people who were there. Jim's extraordinary story telling skill and humor are at the heart of this effort, but it's also an exhaustive account of the band, Gypsy, and all that went on around it. It's a history of a time that is almost slipping away from us.

—Al Zdon

Working Musician

The Story of James Walsh and Gypsy

Bill Graham's Fillmore West in San Francisco, 1970 or 1971. The Marquee advertises Spirit, Poco and Gypsy. It was a premiere West Coast venue for rock and roll bands in that era, and the Grateful Dead were regulars there. (Photo courtesy of Jay Epstein)

Contents

Gypsy performing at the Atlanta Pop Festival in 1970 before a crowd estimated at 350,000-600,000 people. From left, James Walsh, Enrico Rosenbaum, Bill Lordan, Jim Johnson, Doni Larson. The band did several encores. (Photo courtesty Doni Larson)

CHAPTER ONE
ATLANTA POP

So you want to be a rock and roll star?
Then listen now to what I say
Just get an electric guitar
Then take some time and learn how to play

And in a week or two if you make the charts
The girls'll tear you apart.
— "So You Want To Be a Rock and Roll Star"
Chris Hillman and Roger McGuinn, the Byrds, 1967

JAMES WALSH:

When it was time to go on, I remember walking up the steps at the back of the stage, and when I got eye-level with the stage where I could see out, I couldn't see anything but people. It was rolling hills, so some of the people in the back just disappeared. It was a sea of people. My little heart was pounding. I was just little Jimmy Walsh from Northeast Minneapolis.

Our first album had just come out. Our gig at the 1970 Atlanta International Pop Festival was booked through the Heller-Fischel Agency in Los Angeles. They handled several bands, and we were lucky enough to be booked for Atlanta. We flew there. Because of the size of the show, there wasn't a hotel room to be had anywhere. The promoters had set aside some rooms, but you could only stay one day and then you had to move out because another band was coming in that day.

We arrived at the airport, and they told us, "You're going to have a limousine from the airport to the hotel." I thought this was great. They brought up a Cadillac and the guy came over and handed me the keys and said, "There you are." I said, "You're just giving us this Cadillac limousine?" He said, "Yeah, we don't have enough drivers." I quickly grabbed the keys and said, "We're out of here."

So we made our way to the hotel. The guys were smoking hash in the back seat, and I suppose I hit a bump and the hash went down in the seat. Well, we thought, that's no big deal, just fill up the pipe again. The next thing we know, there's billows of smoke coming up from under the seat. The thing with hash is that it doesn't stop burning. They're all screaming "Pull over, pull over, the car's on fire." I'm stoned out of my mind and I'm just saying "What? What?"

So I pulled over, and we poured cans of pop and beer down there and finally got the fire out.

We got to the hotel and there was a guy there to take the limousine back. I don't think we told him about the fire. The next morning we asked how we were going to get to the festival because we didn't have the limousine any more. The next thing we know there's this Ttthhhhuupppppbbbb, and

The official poster of the Atlanta International Pop Festival in 1970. Note "Gypsy" in the lower right corner.

a helicopter landed. They took us down there and flew right over the stage and landed in a field out back. It was pretty cool.

So while we got there in a helicopter, our equipment was still in a truck. There was a way for the trucks to get through, probably in the middle of the night.

Because of the size of the stage and the number of acts, there was a constant flow of trucks in and out. The trailers for the performers were all in two rows behind the stage, about four or five deep. There were two bands in each trailer. The trucks would come up the middle, between the trailers. The roads were muddy and ugly and shitty. They didn't build a ramp for the equipment because they didn't know any better. But they muscled all our stuff up on the stage.

We performed, and it went really well. I can't remember what songs we played, but we performed for about 45 minutes. We used all of our own equipment. They weren't smart enough to have a

Looking out at a sea of people that disappeared into the distance, Gypsy played at the Atlanta Pop fest in 1970. From left, Doni Larson, Jim Johnson, Rico Rosenbaum, Bill Lordan, James Walsh. (Photo courtesy minniepaulmusic.com)

central drum set.

I think we went on at two o'clock in the afternoon and it was really hot. The stages back then were made of plywood, so you've got 85-90 degree sun beating down on that plywood, and you're playing your music. It's hot. When we came off the stage there were these guys who were recording the festival and they were in an air-conditioned trailer. They looked at us and they thought we were going to faint. They said, "Come on in here for a while." We cooled off for a bit.

After we were done playing, everything had to be torn down. So Timmy our road manager and his crew were bringing our stuff off one side, while they were bringing the stuff for the next band up the other side. It was very juvenile in the way they were doing it, but they were winging it. If you build a stage out in a field, they will come.

We went back to our trailer, and we proceeded to get really stoned for a change. We were just celebrating. It wasn't just because we had just played in front of one of the largest crowds in world history. When we finished playing at the Carolina Lanes Bowling Alley and Strip Club in Los Angeles we usually celebrated too.

There's this constant flow of people coming and going all day. Everybody you'd meet was cool. These people are moving in and out. We just kept our trailer, and I don't know how we pulled that off. We were smoking pot and smoking pot and smoking pot. We smoked with John Sebastian who was sharing our trailer.

Somebody brought in this jug of cheap wine. Like a gallon jug. The guy who brought it said he had put 15 hits of mescaline in it, and so I was chugging off that like a wild dog. Eventually, we just stood in the back of the stage and watched all these bands play. It was unbelievable. We stayed there all day, and then the next day, and it just got better and better and better because we were getting higher and higher and higher. I remember I wrecked my shoes in the mud. At the beginning I was dancing around the mud to keep my shoes dry, but by the end of the day I was just slogging through the mud, I didn't care anymore.

So now it's midnight on the second day, and we were still pretty stoned. We're up on the stage, in the back, and Jimi Hendrix starts playing. Now I'm thinking, this is pretty fucking cool. He started two songs and stopped because his band fucked up. We call that a train wreck. He had Mitch Mitchell on drums, but he had his war buddy Billy Cox on bass, and he wasn't very good. They started two songs and stopped. Two train wrecks. I'm thinking, "What the fuck is this?" Then they got into a groove, and it was great.

The lighting was shitty. They had lights coming in from the side, but it was too dim to see anything. In many ways it was just like Woodstock, they weren't ready for anything.

The reaction of the crowd to the bands was humongous. It was a roar. It was almost as loud as the band. So Jimi is playing and he's good, doing his thing. The band was loud and the people were loud, but all of sudden there was this other sound that started to come into our ears, this roaring sound, and it got louder and louder and LOUDER and finally it was all you could hear. Hendrix stopped playing.

It turns out it was Hugh Hefner's Playboy jet, flying right over the stage, and you could see the glow of the engines. It was a black plane, with a white bunny on the back. Zoom, right over the stage. It was like 30 feet over our heads, and it was incredibly loud. It got really quiet really fast once the jet had passed, but then it got really loud again when people realized what it was. I don't know if Hefner got in trouble for that.

That probably straightened me out for a minute.

It was a great time. It was an honor to be there. We stayed in the trailer that night, and in the morning the roads must have opened up because we took a shuttle back to the hotel.

I never think of it as the event it was. It's all kind of a blur. For me, I was a young guy then, maybe 21 years old. We were marching up the steps in the music business, one step at a time, and it just kept falling into place, falling into place.

B Sharp Music was one of the emporiums along Central Avenue, Northeast Minneapolis' main drag. B Sharp was a major provider of band instruments and promotion not only to the Edison-based Coronados but to many bands throughout the Twin Cities. The car in front is a 1960 Plymouth. (Photo courtesy Rick Ballot)

ESSAY

NORTHEAST

By Al Zdon

Minnesota is one of those states in fly-over land. America seems to put most of its eggs in the coastal baskets, while the vast inland territory is only along for the ride.

Minneapolis is the largest city in Minnesota, and like most cities is divided into neighborhoods. One of those neighborhoods is Northeast, so named because in the grid-like pattern of the Mill City, Northeast lies to the north and east of downtown, just across the Mississippi River from the neighborhood that makes up the North Side.

Northeast, sometimes called "Nordeast" as a salute to its ethnic heritage, is itself divided into two regions, the Hill and the Valley. The Valley, close by the river, is the older, more historic section. The Valley was a place of bustling commerce and vibrant immigrant people for a long time while the Hill, moving up and away from the river, was still open fields. The river brought much industry to the neighborhood, including the largest brewery in the city, the Minneapolis Brewing Company, makers of Grain Belt Beer.

The valley was filled with bars, dozens of them, all thriving businesses. It had a large casket company, and scores of large churches, many of them Catholic or Ukrainian Eastern Orthodox. Mostly it was the place where a rowdy bunch of immigrants settled in, escaping from Europe, the old country, ready to make a life in the new world. It was not a melting pot, but more like a huge chef salad with all kinds of distinct flavors and textures, somehow mixing together to make a pleasing whole.

There were Italians and Irish and Polish and Swedes and Norwegians and Ukrainians and Russians and many more. They all had names for each other, and they weren't complimentary. Italians were Wops or Dagos. Irish were Micks, Polish people were Polacks, and so forth. There were no

Northeast was home to the Minneapolis Brewing Company, makers of Grain Belt Beer. A gigantic sign still rises above the Mississippi River in Northeast as a historical artifact. The Minneapolis Brewing Company was closed in 1976 and Grain Belt is no longer made in Minneapolis.

African Americans and there were very few Jews (except for the family that owned Grain Belt). Many of the black Minneapolitans lived on the North Side. A popular joke before political correctness reared its head was that the Lowry Avenue Bridge, over the Mississippi, was the longest bridge in the world because it went from Poland to Africa.

The Valley was also the home of Thomas Alva Edison High School, completed in 1922 and named after the Wizard of Menlo Park. It was a large, three-story building taking up a whole block. Perhaps its most distinctive feature in the 1960s was the interior wall. Because one union washed the walls to a certain height and another union washed them to the ceiling, and one union washed them all the time and the other union only washed them about once a decade, the walls were two-toned, lighter green on the bottom and darker green on the top. The demarcation was called the high water line.

Edison was the educational center of Northeast, and at one point had the distinction of sending the smallest percentage of kids to college of any high school in the state. It served a large area, and boomer-era graduating classes were usually about 450 students. Edison had a proud sports history, particularly in basketball, producing some local legends of the hardcourt including Louie Lopata, Tony Jaros and Don "Swede" Carlson, who later played in the NBA.

After World War II, the second and third generations of those who settled Northeast began to acquire some wealth and moved up the Hill into the pleasant, elm-covered streets.

By 1966, the Hill was nearly all developed and had become a pretty good neighborhood with streets canopied by large trees, homes that were mainly built in the 1940s and 50s, and a wonderful social atmosphere where kids could head out the screen door in the morning and play all day without much concern for their safety. Everybody more or less knew the other families down the block.

It was in this world that James Walsh grew up.

Chapter Two

Growing up

The neighbors are complainin' and the schoolboard called twice today
You know they think he's a fool, and his studies are slipping away
He don't think about nothin' 'cept them rock and roll records to play.

I say it's all right, Pa, let the boy rock and roll
He's got a mind of his own and you know he's got a musical soul
And he's gotta play music and you know we really can't say no.

— "Let the Boy Rock and Roll"
John Sebastian, Joe Butler, Lovin' Spoonful, 1966

James Walsh:

Once upon a time in Never Never Land.

When I was about six, I asked my mom and dad for a drum and they were actually dumb enough to buy me one. That was the biggest mistake they ever made.

We had a piano in the basement, and so I was kind of beginning to teach myself. My mother said, "Well if you're interested in the piano, we should get you some piano lessons." The first teacher said, "I can't teach him anymore. He's already at a level where I can't teach him." So my parents decided to kick it up a notch and they sent me to Arnie Gilbertson, one of the best teachers in Northeast. He was a very good piano player. I should have stayed with Arnie. But I didn't. I didn't like the teaching thing, it was too slow. I seemed to be able to teach myself much faster. Once I got the basic knowledge of the piano, and I was playing drums, I got hooked on this music. So every-

The Walsh Family at home. From left, John, baby Michelle, Betty, James, and Jim. (Photo courtesy Michelle Walsh Armstrong)

thing is sort of self-taught, but this screw kept turning in my head the whole time. It affected everything I did.

My mom was involved with these singing quartets. She took me with her a lot. I suppose she didn't have anywhere to put me. So I remember being in her living room and other living rooms of these women in Northeast and they would practice harmonies. So I got involved with this harmony thing. You know, the structure of songs. And she would take me with her to these Sweet Adeline things over at the University, and I would see the best of the best doing what my mom was doing. They would be little neighborhood groups, the ladies, but they were absolutely good, awesome.

After listening to them, I remember going downstairs to the piano and figuring out what they had just done. One lady would be singing ladadada, the next one ladadada, but higher, and the next woman ladadada, but higher yet. Once I got that in my head, I always had it. I was very young when this was going on.

So I had the snare drum and the piano. Then they bought me some practice pads which I took downstairs and practiced on the drums a lot. I had this feeling.

And then I asked them to get me a tape recorder. So my dad got me a little Sony recorder, and I would tape the music on one side and sing along to it on the other side with a microphone. I always had the bug, I don't know. I should have been a lawyer, what was I thinking? I'd have been a great lawyer.

I was coming home one day when I heard a song on the radio in the car. I can't remember what song it was. I quickly went downstairs and I played it. I was able to figure it out. That kind of inspired me a little bit. I seemed to have a knack right from the beginning. Even today, if I'm in a car and I hear a song on the radio, I can later sit down at the piano and play it. That's weird. That's some kind of a gift. It was better than my English grades.

I got into the summer band thing up at Northeast Junior High. I would rope my snare drum to my back and bike over to the school. My birthday falls on Sept. 6, and I was always on the cusp of staying behind or going ahead. My parents should have held me back — instead of the school holding me back later. I was a sophomore for a couple of years. I was a really good drummer, but I'm not very good anymore. There's too much work drumming. Good God. Especially with Gypsy songs, they're six, eight, 12 minutes long. Holy crap.

I found school boring. I started playing drums in a polka band when I was 12. It was Jerry Zelazny and the Polka All-Stars. They would pick me up on Friday afternoon, and we'd play Friday night, Saturday night and Sunday afternoon, and then we'd come home. I wanted to be a musician. I can't say it was for the glamour. It was something that I really wanted to do, not knowing what level I could take it to. I was always the youngest guy.

In the polka band, they called me "the Kid." I always had to stay on stage. I couldn't go running off to the bar, so now and then they'd bring me a beer or a soda.

I would drive because they would drink. They had a'58 Chevy convertible with a trailer and I'd be driving. We'd get a block from my house, and we'd change drivers so my parents wouldn't know.

Jerry Zelazny grew up in Northeast Minneapolis and graduated from Edison High School in 1960. He played in several bands and then served in the Navy as a gunner's mate and was a Vietnam veteran. A gifted musician, he played in the Dominoes, Jolly Brothers, Mrozinski Brothers, Split Image and Bandit. He won the Minnesota Music Awards Gold Album. He founded Jerry Zelazny and the Polka All-Stars in the early 60s, traveling the state on weekends. He hired a very young drummer named Jim Walsh for his band.

Zelazny died in 2004 at age 61, and his musician friends joined at his wake to play music and honor his memory.

Later in life, I'd talk to my parents about those days. Why would they let me go with these drunken Polacks every weekend? There was one guy in the band named Bill Lucking who was somewhat responsible, and I think they trusted him. But it was an interesting time.

Later on, I was in the marching band at Edison learning from the band director, Mr. Elmo Lunkley.

GROWING UP NORTHEAST

I know everything about Northeast. I love Northeast. I still drive by there. I drive down my alley and I drive by Edison. It's all a very, very good memory for me.

We lived on 35th and Pierce on the corner. We had a nice neighborhood. I had lots of good friends from up and down the block. It was very pleasant. My parents were awesome. We had a pool in our backyard. And so that became the place to meet, and we'd start from there. It was good.

My dad was a policeman and walked the beat on Central Avenue. He was also a coach at Waite Park Elementary School, so I was always with him up there. I played baseball and I played football down at the athletic field. I loved sports, I still love sports, but the music thing was festering in my mind the whole time.

James and John Walsh, with clip-on bow ties firmly in place, posed for this portrait in about 1959. (Photo courtesy Michelle Walsh Armstrong)

I was a terrible kid. I never made my bed. I remember one time, my brother John and I went and got a fishing net out of our sports closet, and we got it to stick out from these shelves. We were shooting baskets into it. And then somebody got the bright idea that if we cut a hole in the bottom of the net we wouldn't have to climb up and retrieve the ball all the time. So we did. We had a great time, and then mom called us for supper, and we just put the net back into the sports closet. We meant to fix it later, although I don't know how. A while later my dad went fishing with one of his buddies, and the other guy gets a large fish and my dad grabbed the net and tried to bring it in. Well, the fish went right through the net. We heard about that one.

And then there was a time when I wanted to go to this party. All the cool neighborhood girls would be there. My dad and mom said no. Well, I was going to this party no matter what. When it got dark, I went up to my bedroom and opened the window. First I threw my party clothes out the window and then I climbed out the window myself. I hung from the window ledge, but I hadn't calculated this very well. I was still a long way from the ground. Finally I just let go, and, whomp, I hit the ground on my back like a ton of bricks. It really hurt. When I finally looked up, I looked over and my dad was sitting in a lawn chair just a few feet away. He knew what I was up to, and he was just waiting. I never made it to that party.

My dad was not very good at technology, and neither am I. One time my dad said he was going to bring something really special home with him. So John and I came home from school, and we were pretty excited. My dad said it had something to do with the phone. We waited, and he finally came home and showed us what he had. It was a long phone cord.

It would let John and I go around the corner and talk on the phone. So from then on, my brother and I were constantly trying to stretch out this phone cord. As soon as you brought the phone back to its base, the line would go fffffffbbbbbbbfffffttttttt and get all tangled up. That was my dad's idea of high technology, a long phone cord.

My parents stopped going to St. Charles for church on Sundays, but they made me and John go. So what we'd do, we'd drive there in my car, I'd stop, and my brother would run inside to get a bulletin. He'd come back to the car and we'd head up to Wynn's or Three Holes drive-in in St. Anthony and sit there for an hour, hour and a half. So when we'd get home, my mom would be waiting. "Did you get your bulletin?"

"Oh, yeah, got it right here."

INTERVIEW

JOHN WALSH

Jim and John Walsh shared a large upstairs bedroom in their Northeast Minneapolis home. John was three years younger. Sister Michelle was the youngest.

"We did everything up there, football, baseball, hockey, even shooting arrows into my dad's knotty pine walls. I'm sure Jim has told you about the time we cut the bottom out of my dad's fishing net so we could use it as a basketball hoop. And then my dad took it fishing."

The Walsh parents, Jim and Betty, were known in the neighborhood as friendly and outgoing, and the traits were passed on to the boys. "Our house was the neighborhood hangout. We had a 16-by-24 foot pool in the backyard, and Friday and Saturdays our yard was the gathering spot.

James holds the ring at his brother's wedding. (Photos courtesy John Walsh)

"Dad got us a go-kart and told us never to drive it when he wasn't there. So, of course, Jim was going up and down the alley, doing spin-outs. He was just peeling into the alley when dad pulled up. That was the end of the go-kart for a while."

The family ate at 5:15 each day. "And we were never late." And on Sundays, through the years, the family always gathered, even after the boys moved out. "We'd get there at noon, play cards, and then we'd eat. Pork roast, sauerkraut, peach dumplings. Oh, it was so good."

In the high school years, John took advantage of the fact that his brother was making good money in a rock and roll band and owned a nice car. "He'd come in late from playing somewhere, and in the morning I'd ask if I could use his car. If he made a noise that sounded positive, I'd take it to school. Then at about 11, I'd hear over the intercom, 'Will John Walsh please bring his brother's keys to the office.' Mom would have to drive him down there."

John played the guitar and drums, but never considered it a career like his brother. "If only I could sing."

Mostly it was great to have an older brother. "We fought all the time, but we were always close. I thought it was great that he had so much success in music, but he never acted like a rock and roll star. He was just a regular guy."

John and his wife, Patty, his high school sweetheart, have two boys and six grandchildren.

James, father Jim, and John Walsh shared a love for golf, and John has won several club championships.

INTERVIEW

GREG 'BOOMER' MORITKO

Greg "Boomer" Moritko grew up just down the street from Jim Walsh and was a childhood friend and also a teammate in local sporting activities including the neighborhood-based Cavell All-Stars.

Greg Moritko and Jim Walsh celebrate a softball victory by the Cavell All-Stars.

Moritko said the neighborhood was safe for kids. "There wasn't much going on. I don't think a door was ever locked. Nobody ever heard of someone having a gun. It's bizarre to think that now kids can't even feel safe at school. We never thought twice." Moritko, who lives near Grand Rapids, Minnesota, frequently comes back to the old stomping grounds. "When we grew up, Northeast was lily white. I like how it's changed. There's so much more ethnicity, it's more exciting."

The Walsh household on the corner was the gathering spot for the neighborhood youth. "His mom and dad were really outgoing. They didn't mind the kids hanging around. They were really fun to talk to.

At a Coronados dance at a local high school. From left: Greg Moritko, Kathy Kiefer, Daryl Moritko, Nancy Manly, James Walsh, Pat Monahan. (Photos courtesy Rick Ballot)

"Yeah, Jim was kind of a troublemaker. But his folks were both on the PTA. So in school, he'd get into trouble, and I'd get blamed. The sixth grade teacher was really a piece of work."

Later, in high school, Moritko saw Walsh play many times. His brother Daryl Moritko, was the road manager of the Coronados for a time. "I saw the Coronados a lot, but bands were playing everywhere in those days. There was no liquor, just venues like the KC Halls. When they became Gypsy, they didn't go the Chicago route, they were more like King Crimson, more jazzy, more of a unique style."

He said there were times when just he and Jim would gather at the piano in the Walsh basement and sing some of the current songs. "I taught him everything he knows about music," said

Moritko, tongue in cheek.

Chuck Berry in 1957. (Public domain)

ESSAY

FROM W.C. HANDY TO GARAGE BANDS

By Al Zdon

So where did rock and roll come from? When did it start?

Ed Ward, who wrote *The History of Rock and Roll*, said some people chronologically pin it down to one month and one year: May, 1955. Among other things, that was when Bill Haley's "Rock Around the Clock" began exploding up the pop charts. Haley had recorded the song the year before, but it had not caught on. Only when the movie "Rebel Without a Cause" came out and used the song over the opening credits, did it explode. Haley and his Comets appeared on the Milton Berle television show in May, the first rock band on national TV, and the song became the first rock and roll effort to top the Billboard popular music charts in July.

How, you may wonder, did this song, done by a 31-year-old white guy, usher in the rock and roll era? I, for one, don't think of Bill Haley when I think of early rock and roll. I think of black musicians, doo wop, and girl groups. Even at that time, I thought Bill Haley was kind of corny, and way too old to be singing my music.

So, yes, it's kind of complicated. But let's try to go back to the real roots of rock and roll, at least in the 20th Century.

Let's start with William Christopher Handy, a black musician some call the "Father of the Blues." W.C. Handy tried various professions including carpentry, shoemaking and plastering, but he couldn't stop trying to teach himself how to play the cornet. He worked on a "shovel brigade" in the local steel mill, and his comrades would beat their shovels on the ground in complex rhythms, rhythms that Handy said were at the heart of the Blues. Once in 1903 at a railroad station in Tutwiler, Mississippi, Handy said he heard a black musician sitting on the platform play a slide guitar using a knife. He said it affected him deeply.

W.C. Handy in 1949. Handy brought black music into the mainstream of American music. (World Wide Photos, public domain)

In 1909, he and his band moved to Memphis and he wrote his first "hit:" "The Memphis Blues." He worked at his music, bringing in the sound of black folk music, along with what came to be known as "blues notes." In 1914, he published the "St. Louis Blues" and "Beale Street Blues." His repertoire of songs soon became fodder for emerging jazz bands of the time. Oddly enough, Handy's music was mostly performed by white bands and combos. Still, he brought rural American black music to the Great American Songbook.

The 1920s was still a time when most of the music in America was still heard in parlours or on the front porch. The music was played at work, in the church, at parties. It was basically folk music because it was played by the folks. Minstrel shows and medicine shows spread the music from city to city throughout the nation.

The invention of the phonograph and the increase in sheet music sales also spread the music, creating a popular music in the country. If one musician did something that caught on with the people, a dozen other musicians were sure to follow. There was plenty of leeway for musicians to add their own licks or words. Guitars and pianos were popular.

Ralph Peer grew up in Missouri and as a young man worked with Columbia Records in Kansas City. His talent at finding music landed him a job with Okey Records in New York, and he did pioneering work in recording blues songs and the first commercial recordings made in New Orleans. He did early work in recording country music.

In 1927, at age 35, he took his portable recording equipment to Bristol, Tennessee, looking for talent. At this time, he was working for the Victor Talking Machine Company and was paid a dollar a year by the company. Instead of a salary, he owned the rights to all the music he found, and he paid the musicians a royalty based on sales. This is still a common practice in the business.

Jimmie Rodgers, the Singing Brakeman, and perhaps the first great singer-songwriter, in 1931. (Victor Talking Machine Company, public domain)

The Carter Family — A.P., Maybelle and Sara —in 1927, the year they auditioned with Ralph Peer. (Victor Talking Machine Company, public domain)

At Bristol, he advertised in the newspaper for talent and between July 25 and August 5, he held sessions on the third floor of a hat and glove warehouse. The ads didn't generate much interest, but a newspaper story about the amount of royalties a local musician had received a year earlier plus the $100 a day pay for recording drew people from all over. Peer recorded 76 songs by 19 different artists or groups.

Two of those artists were Jimmie Rodgers, later known as the "yodeling brakeman" and the Carter Family, truly the first family of country music. The sessions have been described as the "big bang" of country music.

The Carters, with Sara singing lead and cousin Maybelle on guitar, had success from that first recording session. Legend has it that A.P. Carter, Sara's husband, sought out and married her because of her wonderful voice. It was A.P. that convinced these down-home women to travel all day to Bristol to make their first recording. In the next three years, the family sold 300,000 records, and A.P. traveled the region looking for new songs.

Along the way, they set the standard for country groups, when country really meant country. Songs like "Wabash Cannonball," "Can the Circle Be Unbroken," and "Keep on the Sunny Side," are classics.

Jimmie Rodgers was probably America's first singer-songwriter recording star. Jimmie had a pen-

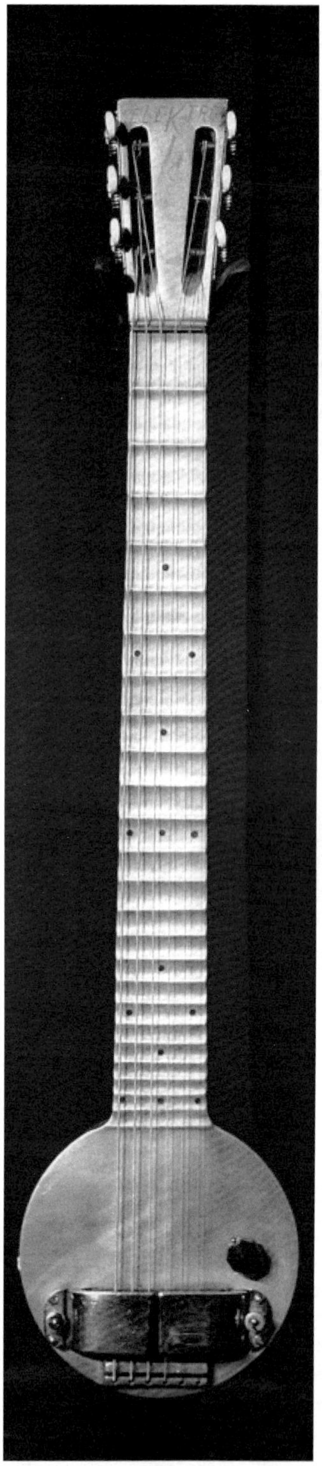

chant for entertaining, and twice, at age 13, he organized traveling musical shows only to be brought home by his father. He worked as a water boy for a regional railroad, and was exposed to African-American music early on. He later became a brakeman.

Rodgers was enthusiastic about recording and traveled to New York for sessions. He enlisted his sister-in-law, Elsie McWilliams to write some new songs for him. She became his long-time songwriting partner. He recorded "Blue Yodel" during one session, and it sold a half million copies. Rodgers said he learned to yodel from listening to a Swiss group singing at a church.

He continued to record and toured with Will Rogers. By 1932, the Yodeling Brakeman was probably the top recording artist in the nation. In 1933, he returned to New York for more recordings, but his tuberculosis had become much worse due to his incessant traveling. He died in a New York hotel two days after completing the session. He was 35. He brought the Blues to the common people, and he was an influence on generations of musicians to come.

American music from the 1920s on, and to a certain degree prior to that, took on a business framework that still exists. The development of the Victrola, the proliferation of radios, recording sessions, rights and royalties, music venues, and large companies trying to make a buck from someone's talent, created a capitalist side to music.

It's interesting that during the 20s, recording artists often had complete control over what they did in the "studio." If Maybelle Carter wanted to play the melody on the bass strings and use her index finger to fill out the rhythm, nobody was going to stop her. This was how she played. Some say her style moved the guitar from strictly a rhythm instrument to a lead instrument, and we all know what that led to.

That kind of artistic control did not become the norm again until the 1960s with the explosion of rock and roll, and the demand by artists to create their own sound, to experiment, to invent.

The Electro, or "Frying Pan," considered by many to be the first commericial electric guitar. (Museum of Making Music at English Wikipedia)

One other important thing happened in the early 1930s. The Electro-String Instrument Corporation, listening to its customers, the musicians, developed a steel guitar with an electromagnetic pickup. It was an odd instrument, long with a tiny, circular body on the end. It was called the "frying pan." The need for a louder guitar was driven by jazz musicians, who wanted every note to be heard, and by orchestra guitarists who were getting drowned out as the bands got larger.

Gibson got into the electric guitar business in 1936, and Les Paul developed his solid body guitar in 1942. Called "the log," it was a 4x4 piece of lumber with strings and a pickup. The design improved and the 1952 Gibson Les Paul model was considered a breakthrough. In the end, the electric guitar became a basic instrument for rock and roll, jazz, country and other types of music. It should be noted that Les Paul also invented multitracking, a staple of rock recording.

Alan Freed was generally credited with creating the term "rock and roll." He once played Maybellene for two hours straight to promote it on his radio station. (TV-Radio Mirror, public domain)

The 1950s saw a boom in record sales, radio was popular, and television was just hitting the scene. The band era created ballrooms in nearly every city where people could listen to music and dance — later ideal venues for rock and roll bands and teenagers. And, of course, there were jukeboxes at the corner bar or pizza palace.

You could discuss forever how all the elements from W.C. Handy to Jimmie Rodgers to the Carter Family to Louis Armstrong to Glenn Miller to T-Bone Walker to Chuck Berry to Sister Rosetta Tharp meshed to become rock and roll. Essentially what was happening was that the various streams of black music started to become popular with white people. This, of course, goes way back to minstrel shows and jazz clubs and big bands. But what happened in the 1950s was that the music became dominant with white teenagers, often to the chagrin or dismay of their parents.

Sure, there was still a lot of "How Much Is That Doggie in the Window?" in the early 50s, but now you could also buy Big Mama Thornton singing "Hound Dog," yes the same song that Elvis covered in 1956. Big Mama's version is much better.

And just to take that one song as an example, you might think it's a song that came fully realized from Beale Street or a Chicago honkytonk. Actually the song was written by Jerry Lieber and Mike Stoller, two Jewish kids from the East Coast who met and began writing songs in Los Angeles.

They loved rhythm and blues, and started cranking out songs like "Kansas City," "Charlie Brown," "Yakety Yak," "Stand by Me," and "Love Potion Number Nine." Two white Jewish kids were writing songs for black performers that were sold to white teenage audiences.

Alan Freed was born in 1921 and grew up in Ohio. He is often credited with popularizing the term "rock and roll" which in historical terms meant a ship moving through the waves and in black history meant sexual intercourse. He quite accurately said rock and roll "is a river of music which has absorbed many streams: rhythm and blues, jazz, ragtime, cowboy songs, folk songs. All have contributed to the big beat."

Let's pick up one more thread before we get back to 1955. In 1949, RCA issued its first seven-inch 45 rpm disk. It had a song on each side and was affordable to teens at the record store. Of course, you had to have a 45 player. Columbia had released the first 33 1/3 12 inch vinyl record in 1948. These technological improvements were ideal for rock and roll. The 45s created a top 40 culture and market that was extraordinarily sensitive to what young people wanted to hear. The larger "album" allowed songs to be grouped on a single piece of vinyl. Both were great sound improvements over the brittle 78 rpms that were the industry standard for many years.

So, in 1955, we have Bill Haley, but mainly we have this huge door swinging open and allowing rock and roll to come flooding through. Maybe in the 1930s, teens didn't have much spending power or couldn't use what they had for extraneous buying, but in the 50s, America was flush with money and 69 cents for that new 45 was in nearly everybody's reach.

Through this door marched a small army of black musicians and some whities too: Chuck Berry, Bo Diddley, Little Richard, Jerry Lee Lewis, Elvis Presley, and Fats Domino. Chuck Berry's "Maybellene" came out in 1955, as did "Earth Angel" by the Penguins, "Ain't that a Shame" by Fats, and "Only You" by the Platters.

It was "Maybellene" that many consider the ultimate rock and roll breakthrough song, and it was the second best selling pop song of the year behind "Rock Around the Clock." The song features a driving beat, unrequited love, fast cars, and Berry's distorted lead guitar solo. It had everything. And here's the funny part, Berry had borrowed the song from an old Bob Wills' western swing song called "Ida Red." Leonard Chess, the proprietor of Chess Records, encouraged Berry to change the name and lyrics, and the rest is history. If the guitar lick sounds a little tired, it may be because the band had to use 36 takes to get the song right.

There was also the phenomenon of Elvis Presley, a truck driver from Memphis who grew up listening to black music of both the secular and spiritual kind, and used his astonishing voice and bodily gyrations to bring that sound and power to teenage girls. A newspaper at the time said he was a "white boy with black hips."

Little Richard has been called the "architect of rock and roll," and his driving, tuneful songs like "Tutti Frutti" and "Long Tall Sally" zoomed up the pop charts. He was one of the most imitated of the early pioneers.

Buddy Holly changed his band's specialty from country to rock and roll and brought an elevated level of songwriting. His first album was overproduced and went nowhere, but he got control of the studio after that and produced such songs as "Peggy Sue" and "That'll be the Day." Holly's death in a plane crash in Iowa in 1959, along with the Big Bopper and Ritchie Valens, is considered by some a symbolic end to this first phase of rock and roll, and was the subject of Don McLean's "Bye, Bye Miss American Pie."

In truth, though, as the 60s came along, rock and roll was just getting started. This era was when much of the dynamics of recording were advanced by such people as Phil Spector and his "wall of sound" and Berry Gordy's Motown Sound. We could do a whole book on that, and I'm sure somebody has, but let's move on to the British Invasion.

The Beatles were the superstars, but they weren't the only group from England to be part of the invasion. The Searchers, The Dave Clark Five, the Kinks, Chad and Jeremy, Jerry and the Pacemakers, the Animals, Dusty Springfield, Peter and Gordon, and Billy J. Kramer and the Dakotas all graced the top 100. Why? The easy answer is they created good music that teenagers wanted to hear. In some cases, especially the Beatles, they took American black music and did their best. English people singing black rock and roll, rhythm and blues, and even gospel was a witch's brew of extraordinary power and importance.

The Beach Boys and other California bands were the answer to the Brits. The brilliant harmonies — descended from the Four Freshmen and the doo-wop bands — stood out. For a time, Brian Wilson's Beach Boy albums were taking on the Beatles's efforts punch for punch.

And one more tile for this mosiac is folk music. From Woody Guthrie in the 30s and 40s to Pete Seeger to the Weavers in the 40s and 50s to the new purveyors of folk — Peter, Paul and Mary, the Kingston Trio, the New Christy Minstrels, Donovan, Joan Baez, Joni Mitchell, Judy Collins, Arlo Guthrie — folk music was picking up some serious steam.

Oh, and then there was this guy, Bob Dylan, the only musician to win the Nobel Prize for literature. Growing up in the remote mining country of northern Minnesota, he brought poetry and a message to his songs. At first he was topically political, but after stirring up the souls of his listeners to fight for freedom and peace and love and insight, he actually broadened his vision. His songs in the 2020s still break new ground.

Dylan chose Woody Guthrie as his hero. Guthrie was the great folk singer who rose out of Oklahoma and the Dust Bowl to pen some of the greatest songs in that great American song book. It was the folk music movement in the 60s from which Dylan emerged. The young people were seeking music that had depth, that was singable and playable, that had history, and even that elusive message.

I remember in the late 60s and early 70s someone would be talking about a new album they heard. And the other person in the conversation would respond, "but what do they have to say?" What an artist had to say was the crucial element.

Dylan and the Beatles and hundreds more said something to that generation that was trying to escape what they perceived as the straightjacket of the prior generation. But the music wasn't just coming from major record labels and from the media. It was coming from the people, the young people.

It's been estimated that there were from 350 to 500 garage bands in the Twin Cities in the early

1960s.

Some of these bands worked their way out of the garage and into the local gymnasiums for sock hops and junior high dances. Some worked their way from the hops to local music venues, often Knights of Columbus or American Legion or Masonic halls. A few advanced to the point of playing regularly at the ballrooms in the cities and around the state. In Minnesota a very few created music that ended up on the Billboard national charts. Some of these were the Trashmen's "Surfin' Bird," the Castaways "Liar, Liar," the Accents, "Why," and the Gestures, "Run, Run, Run."

As rock and roll music spread through the young people of America in the early 60s, teenagers with a musical bent sometimes tried to put a group together. The originator was sometimes a guitarist. Drummers sometimes came from the high school band. Bass players sometimes were somebody's friend who didn't play an instrument.

If they worked really hard and practiced and practiced and practiced, and had some natural talent, they might work their way from the oily floors of the garage onto a bandstand. Almost all the bands in America and England emerged from the grassroots, from the people. It was one of the distinguishing features of the rock and roll band.

They were us.

Jim Walsh sings out with the Coronados, circa 1964. Rick Ballot is on drums. (Photo courtesy Jan Rangel)

The Coronados, about 1964. There were no portable keyboards at the time, and so James Walsh is posing with a Cordovox, an accordian that could be plugged in. Ballot, the drummer, was the leader of the band. Walsh was three or four years younger than the other band members, but also the lead singer. From left: Walsh, Fred Draper, Ballot, Larry Bruhjell, Drew Pederson, John Kaminski. (Photo courtesy Rick Ballot)

CHAPTER THREE

CORONADOS, HOT HALF DOZEN

It's like a heat wave
Burning in my heart (It's like a heat wave)
I can't keep from crying (It's like a heat wave)
It's tearing me apart.
— "Heat Wave," 1966, The Hot Half Dozen
Lamont Dozier, Brian Holland, Eddie Holland

JAMES WALSH:

My neighborhood friend Rick Ballot, who was four years older than me, had a band called the Coronados. I would go down to his house when they were practicing, and I would get in the window well and listen. In those days, I was small enough to get into the window well. I'd go down there all the time. They knew I was there. Well, one time Rick signaled me to come into the house. He said, "Do you know these songs?" I said, "Yeah, I know these songs." He said, "Well, can you sing these songs?" I said, "I think so."

I don't think Rick knew I could sing, but they had this job that weekend and they were desperate. These were not hard songs, they were easy songs like "Louie, Louie." It didn't take a lot of study.

My parents let me go because they trusted Rick Ballot. He was kind of the Eagle Scout on the block. That was a big deal. He was kind of a mentor of mine. He took me under his wing. When I joined the Coronados, without knowing it, I was the best singer. In a very short period of time, I became *the* singer. I had everything a band could want at that time. I was good looking, I was a small, little guy.

The Coronados play a New Year's Eve party about 1964. (Photo courtesy Rick Ballot)

The Coronados evolved into the Hot Half Dozen and both the music and suits got better. The Hot Half Dozen began to play the same venues as the other top bands in town, and they recorded for SOMA records and had a regional hit with "Heat Wave." From left: James Walsh, now with his Farfisa keyboard, George Nowell, Fred Draper, Rick Ballot, Ron Geslin, Larry Brujhell. (Photo courtesy James Walsh)

schnapps. It was something the fraternity required of the guys in the band who were playing at their digs. I just went along with the party. I got home at 3:30 in the morning, drunk.

My parents were both sitting up at the kitchen table waiting for me. It took me a couple of weeks to get out of that trouble. I kind of didn't play with them for a while after that.

We auditioned for the Silver Skate Roller Rink in North St. Paul. It was a big dance place, and the main band there was Gregory Dee and the Avanties. We went over there and played, and the guy said, "I like you guys. You're good. But I won't hire you unless you have an organ." He said "organ" and Rick Ballot's head went right to me. The organ they had at the rink was a Hammond M1. I didn't even know how to turn it on. So the guy turned it on for me, and I scuffled through a couple songs. The guy said, "Okay, I'll hire you guys." So, we got all excited except for the fact that we didn't have an organ. They only had the Hammond at the Silver Skate because it was a roller rink. The Avanties used to use it.

That's when we decided I was officially going to be in the band. We went down to B Sharp Music on Central Avenue which was owned by Jim Lopes. There were no compact organs then. It was either a big organ or an accordion. Jim Lopes had an accordion and he said he'd let us use it or rent it, I can't remember what it was. It was electronic with an amp. I didn't have to pump it. We did that for a while.
The guys in the band were Rick Bal-

It wasn't all music. Walsh and Ballot were also part of the Cavell All-Stars softball team, named after the city park in the neighborhood. (Photo courtesy Rick Ballot)

Jim Lopes, the proprietor of B Sharp Music, was a major player in the Twin Cities' rock scene of the 1960s. Bands would not only hang out at the Central Avenue store, but would work together with Lopes on promotions. Lopes let the Coronados use a new Farfisa compact keyboard, the first on the market, and soon other bands were knocking at the door. He once gave a guitar to the Beatles. Lopes paid for painting various bands' name on their buses and vans. (Photo courtesy minniepaulmusic.com)

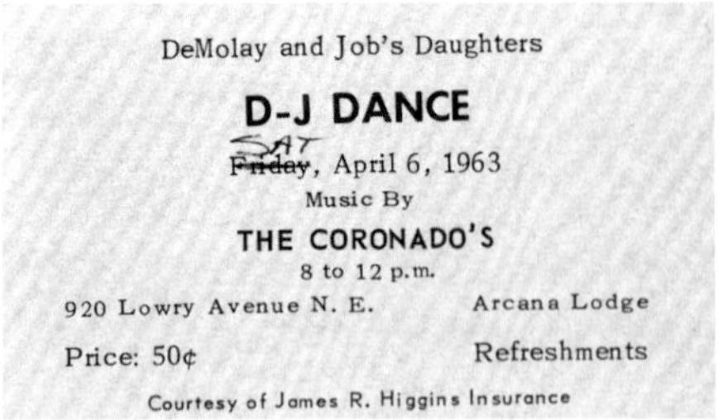

DeMolay and Job's Daughters

D-J DANCE

~~Friday~~ SAT, April 6, 1963

Music By

THE CORONADO'S

8 to 12 p.m.

920 Lowry Avenue N. E. — Arcana Lodge

Price: 50¢ — Refreshments

Courtesy of James R. Higgins Insurance

The Arcana Lodge was a Masonic hall on Central Avenue, and a popular spot for teen dances.

The Standard Club in Minneapolis was another hot spot for bands.

James Walsh appeared pensive after a Coronados gig.

the CORONADOS

ST. 1-4295

SPONSORED BY

B# Music Store

4050 CENTRAL AVE.

SU 8-9249

LESSONS, SALES, REPAIRS

Franchised Dealer of —

FENDER, GIBSON, AMPEG

B Sharp provided many of the instruments for Minneapolis bands. (All photos on these two pages courtesy Rick Ballot)

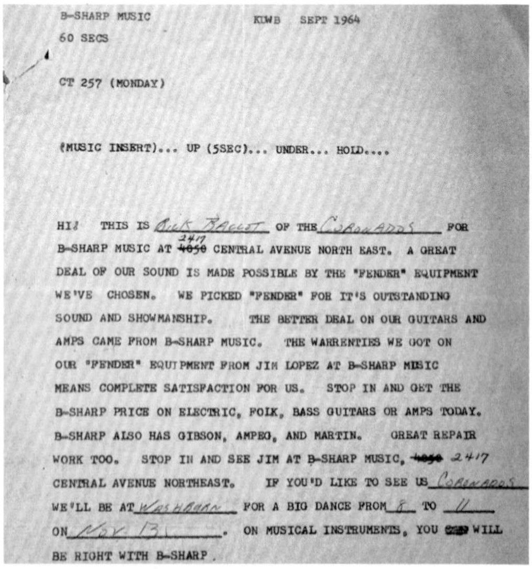

B-SHARP MUSIC — KDWB SEPT 1964

60 SECS

CT 257 (MONDAY)

(MUSIC INSERT)... UP (5SEC)... UNDER... HOLD....

HI! THIS IS Rick Ballot OF THE Coronados FOR B-SHARP MUSIC AT ~~4050~~ 2417 CENTRAL AVENUE NORTH EAST. A GREAT DEAL OF OUR SOUND IS MADE POSSIBLE BY THE "FENDER" EQUIPMENT WE'VE CHOSEN. WE PICKED "FENDER" FOR IT'S OUTSTANDING SOUND AND SHOWMANSHIP. THE BETTER DEAL ON OUR GUITARS AND AMPS CAME FROM B-SHARP MUSIC. THE WARRENTIES WE GOT ON OUR "FENDER" EQUIPMENT FROM JIM LOPEZ AT B-SHARP MUSIC MEANS COMPLETE SATISFACTION FOR US. STOP IN AND GET THE B-SHARP PRICE ON ELECTRIC, FOLK, BASS GUITARS OR AMPS TODAY. B-SHARP ALSO HAS GIBSON, AMPEG, AND MARTIN. GREAT REPAIR WORK TOO. STOP IN AND SEE JIM AT B-SHARP MUSIC, ~~4050~~ 2417 CENTRAL AVENUE NORTHEAST. IF YOU'D LIKE TO SEE US Coronados WE'LL BE AT Washburn FOR A BIG DANCE FROM 8 TO 11 ON Nov. 13. ON MUSICAL INSTRUMENTS, YOU WILL BE RIGHT WITH B-SHARP.

B Sharp would advertise bands and their products on KDWB. This is a form script with the Coronados band filled in.

lot, Jeff Brenda, Larry Bruhjell, John Kaminski, Fred Draper and me. I think they were all Northeast guys.

I was the smallest guy in the band, but now I've got that accordion and I'm as big as any three guys in the band. It was hilarious.

We would go out and play and play and play. Then one day, we got a call from Jim Lopes. He said, come on down here to B Sharp, I've got something. We went down and sitting in his office was a Farfisa organ which was the first compact organ. "I want you guys to have this, and I want you guys to play it." I don't know how much it cost, maybe 99 bucks or something. But that Farfisa was the first portable organ that you could take out and play.

We evolved into the Hot Half Dozen. That was a pretty successful band. We played for a year or so. Rick Ballot and I took a couple of people from the Coronados, and made the new band. That turned out to be a better band because we had better musicians. Dick Shapiro got involved with us. He and Bill Diehl had an agency called the Central Booking Agency. They came out to hear us play, so we signed with them. The big bands were the Underbeats, Gregory Dee and the Avanties, the Accents and the Chancellors. The Hot Half Dozen was kind of moving up the ladder, starting to play at the same places.

The Hot Half Dozen began playing some of the larger venues. Note the caution at the bottom: "Girls: No Slacks."

By 1966, the KC Hall in Fridley was a major venue for the top bands in the Twin Cities.

Rick Ballot and James Walsh as part of the Coronados. (Photos courtesy Rick Ballot)

INTERVIEW

RICK BALLOT

By Al Zdon

Rick Ballot, the founder of the Coronados rock and roll band of 1960s fame, recalls the time he was driving the band back from a gig in western Minnesota.

He looked in the rearview mirror and something was wrong. He looked again, and sure enough there was something very wrong. The trailer, with all the band's equipment, was not behind the vehicle.

"I woke up all the other guys and I said, 'We lost the trailer.' They all woke up and gave me a lot of shit. 'You dumb ass, what did you do with the trailer? Quit fooling around.' I said, 'No, the trailer's gone. I think it's in the ditch.' They all looked around and there was no trailer."

The Coronados trailer before it disappeared on the highway after a gig.

Ballot turned the car around, and sure enough, down the road was the trailer, crumpled up in a ditch. It had been hitched to the car's steel rear bumper, and somebody hadn't done a very good job of securing it.

"It was busted all to hell. We got all the crumpled equipment into the car, I don't know how we did that, and drove home. The next day we had to go back and get the trailer."

Playing in a band that got jobs all over the Twin Cities and Minnesota perhaps wasn't all the glamour some people may have thought.

———

Rick Ballot grew up in Northeast Minneapolis on 34th and Buchanan. When he attended Northeast Junior High School in seventh grade, the school told him he had a choice of being in the choir or being in the band. "Knowing how well I sing, that was a no brainer." He decided he'd be a drummer.

"I'd always liked drumming. At home I'd take a metal waste basket, turn it upside down, and use a couple of pencils, eraser side down, to drum. I'd put a key chain on the top of the basket to get a snare drum sound."

He became a drummer in the junior high school band, and by the time he got to Edison High School, he was the lead drummer. A pretty good athlete, he also participated in football, wrestling and track, where he ran the hurdles. "I had the best form of all the hurdlers, and I was also the slowest."

A problem for the band at Edison High School was at the football games. "The band director would make all the football players play in the band at halftime. They had some kind of meeting later and decided that the football players needed to concentrate on football during the games, and so we didn't have to play at halftime after that."

Ballot was walking down the hallway at Edison one day in 1961when he was approached by a couple of kids he didn't know. One of them, Jeff Brenda, told him they were starting a rock and roll band, and they needed a drummer and they asked him if he'd be interested. He said he was very interested.

The trouble was that he didn't have a drum kit. "I begged my mother and father for a set of drums, and they finally gave in. Jim Walsh senior, Jim Walsh's dad, who lived down the block, said he might be able to get a set cheap. We went to some warehouse in St. Paul and got the drums at a door in the back. Who knows where they came from. It was a set of Ludwigs."

"By that time, I knew what the hands of a drummer were supposed to do, and the feet came later."

In those early days, people came and went in the band. They would practice at one of their houses, or in Ballot's grandmother's basement, across the alley from his house. The original band had Ballot on drums, Larry Bruhjell and Brenda on guitars, John Kaminski on bass and later on added a saxophone player, Fred Draper. Guitarist Drew Pederson joined later.

An early version of the Coronados playing in somebody's basement. (Photo courtesy Rick Ballot)

What Ballot was missing was a cymbal, and he went down to B-Sharp Music which was then at 41st and Central in Northeast Minneapolis and ordered a 22-inch Zildjian cymbal from a catalog. "That was the first piece of drum equipment that B-Sharp ever sold." When the original B Sharp burned down, they moved to 24th and Central and became a haven for young musicians. "Pretty soon everybody was buying from B-Sharp, and musicians were always hanging around, especially on Saturday afternoons. You got to know all the guys in the bands around the area. It was a great scene."

The Coronados played at fraternity and sorority houses at the University of Minnesota, at Northeast Junior High School dances, and at other places up and down Central Avenue, the main drag of Northeast.

When they would practice at his grandmother's house, there was a window well that looked into where they were playing. Soon, nearly every time they played, they'd see somebody sitting in the well taking it all in. It was little Jimmy Walsh from down the block.

"We all knew he was there. We'd say, 'Look at that dumbass up there watching us.' One day, we had a gig at a frat house and we needed a singer, and I went outside and asked him if he knew all the lyrics to the songs. I don't know how I knew he could sing."

Walsh was a drummer himself, and so he had no real place in the band. "We just had him hold a guitar and pretend like he was playing. But all he was doing is singing. He was our lead singer right from the start."

"We figured out pretty soon that we needed Jim to be on keyboards. He didn't claim to be a piano player, but I knew he had an old upright in his basement, and I knew he could play it."

The band went down to B-Sharp to see about a portable keyboard. "But all Jim Lopes had was a Cordovox electric accordion. He said we could use it. But you know, it didn't look good, and Jim didn't like playing it. But we would borrow it every weekend. It was kind of a bummer."

But a few months later, Lopes called the band and said he had the first compact keyboard on the market, a Farfisa. "I think he just let us use it. But pretty soon other bands saw it, and they were all going down to B-Sharp to buy one."

The Coronados played the Teen Center at the Minnesota State Fair, and one of the strongest parts of their act was when Drew Pederson would play an ensemble of surf instrumentals on his guitar. On this occasion, Dick Shapiro and Ira Heilicher, two young guys who had just formed a booking agency, were in the audience.

Drew Pederson

"So Drew starts his instrumental and just as he's getting going, he drops his pick. He can't pick it up, so he keeps strumming using his thumb. It's a long piece, and so pretty soon he cuts his thumb and he starts bleeding. And pretty soon he's bleeding all down his hand and all over his Stratocaster.

"Shapiro and Heilicher were in the front row, and they couldn't believe it. They came up to us afterward and asked me, 'Can that guitar player do that every night?' I said I didn't think so. But they still liked the band."

Path Music, later the Central Booking Agency, started to book the Coronados all over the state.

The Coronados opened for many national acts in the coming years. They played at Dayton's 8th Floor auditorium several times, and later as the Hot Half Dozen once opened for the Yardbirds.

One time, at the Marigold Ballroom, they opened for the Kingsmen, a group out of Portland who

Rock 'n' Roll Band Bookers Started on a Modest Scale

By JERRY KIRSHENBAUM
Minneapolis Tribune Staff Writer

When Richard Shapiro and Ira Heilicher started out, it was just a noisy little business venture.

They began booking rock 'n' roll bands in the teen-age market — fraternity parties, dance halls, school bashes and like that.

It was only later that the two young businessmen recognized monumental implications for the entire community.

"MINNEAPOLIS could be another Nashville," said Shapiro, 18, 4440 W. 25th St., St. Louis Park.

"It could rival Southern California — on a small scale, of course," said Heilicher, 18, 4241 Basswood Road, St. Louis Park.

In other words, city fathers, our town could become a third national center for the creation and appreciation of rock 'n' roll.

Shapiro and Heilicher are doing their part.

THE TWO University of Minnesota freshmen are booking agents for some 35 bands, 6 of them on an exclusive basis.

They find work, they say, for about 18 bands a week, most of which dispense pulsating rhythms and deafening electronic sounds that the younger set consumes as music.

"Minneapolis is already getting a national reputation," said Shapiro, crediting teen-agers for demanding "good talent" and local bands for providing it.

SOME PARENTS believe inadequate noise ordinances might also be a factor.

As Shapiro tells it, his involvement in booking began two years ago when he went to visit a high school friend hospitalized with a broken nose suffered in a scuffle over a girl.

In a building near the hospital parking lot, he heard a rock 'n' roll group "and it sounded great."

"So I went inside, introduced myself and offered to get them a job at a high school fraternity dance. They said they weren't working too much, so . . ."

A WORKING arrangement developed. But one night just before an engagement, two band members called in sick.

Shapiro went to Heilicher for help. Together they found a couple of fellows to fill in on a one-night basis.

"If I get any money out of this, I'll split it with you," Shapiro told his friend.

Heilicher replied: "You should find another group to fill in if something like this ever happens again."

Thus, Path Musical Productions Co. roared into existence.

The first new band contacted was the Chancellors, today a name to conjure with in some circles, what with the group's recording of "Little Latin Lupe Lu" and all.

(The Chancellors originally were called the Continentals. But no sooner did Heilicher and Shapiro take over than a group by the same name threatened lawsuit.

(Said Shapiro: "We conferred for maybe a second about whether to take it to court. We decided to change the name.")

THEIR BANDS, the two associates said, hire out for \$70 to \$250 an engagement, depending on the particular booking and the band's popularity. Heilicher and Shapiro take a standard 10 per cent fee.

They'll give it all up, said Shapiro, "if it ever starts interfering with our school work." Meanwhile, he added, "we have developed the strongest ears in town."

Much of the booking of Twin City Bands was done by Ira Heilicher and Richard Shapiro.

Jim Walsh on keyboards. (Photo courtesy Rick Ballot)

had a mega hit with "Louie, Louie," which almost every garage band in America covered over the years.

"We did our set, but the Kingsmen weren't there. And time went by. And finally, they came rolling in and they were drunk. I watched the drummer set up his kit, and I couldn't believe it. The Marigold had these beautiful wooden floors, and once this guy had his bass drum in place he kept it from moving by pulling out a mallet and by driving in a four-inch railroad spike into the stage. Wham, wham, wham.

"One of the other guys in our band wondered if we should tell the manager and I said, 'Only if he asks about the big hole in the floor.'"

Since the trailer idea hadn't worked so well, Ballot went shopping for a bus and found one – a beautiful 1958 Volkswagen bus that could top out at 56 miles an hour on the highway. Two band members would sit in the front, and the rest would sit behind the equipment in the back, where there was no heating.

"I did most of the driving, but Jeff Brenda liked to drive too. He came up with this idea that we could draft behind a semi-truck on the highway and the truck would pull us along at a better rate of speed. Walsh would sit in the passenger seat and it was his job to keep his eye on the truck's brake lights. He didn't like that too much.

"One time we were on our way down 169, and I was driving a car and Jeff was somewhere behind us with the bus. We pulled over at a drive-in at St. Peter to get something to eat, and we were keeping an eye out for the bus. Pretty soon, we saw this big semi barreling down the road, and somebody said, 'I bet the bus is right behind it.'

"Sure enough, as the truck flew by, there was the bus about two feet from the rear bumper, and Jim was sitting up straight in the seat, his

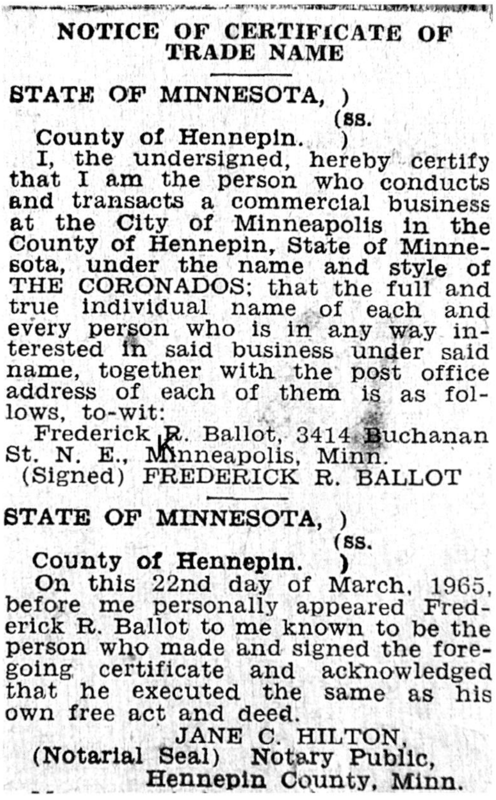

NOTICE OF CERTIFICATE OF TRADE NAME

STATE OF MINNESOTA,)
(ss.
County of Hennepin.)

I, the undersigned, hereby certify that I am the person who conducts and transacts a commercial business at the City of Minneapolis in the County of Hennepin, State of Minnesota, under the name and style of THE CORONADOS; that the full and true individual name of each and every person who is in any way interested in said business under said name, together with the post office address of each of them is as follows, to-wit:

Frederick R. Ballot, 3414 Buchanan St. N. E., Minneapolis, Minn.

(Signed) FREDERICK R. BALLOT

STATE OF MINNESOTA,)
(ss.
County of Hennepin.)

On this 22nd day of March, 1965, before me personally appeared Frederick R. Ballot to me known to be the person who made and signed the foregoing certificate and acknowledged that he executed the same as his own free act and deed.

JANE C. HILTON,
(Notarial Seal) Notary Public,
Hennepin County, Minn.

Ballot had the Coronados name officially registered as a trade name in 1965.

Could young Jimmy Walsh dunk? The camera never lies.

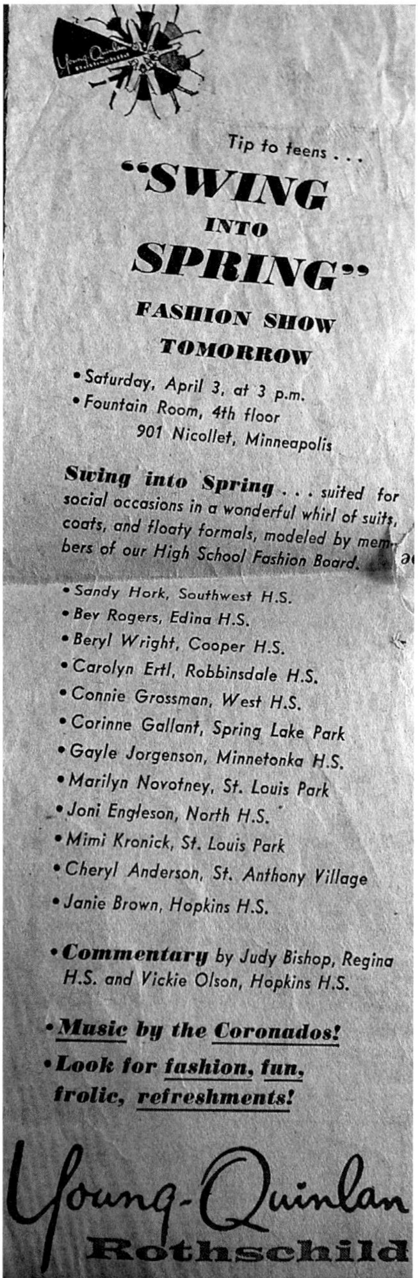

It wasn't all sock hops and basement parties for the Coronados. They also did fashion shows. (All photos courtesy Rick Ballot)

Rick Ballot's head was front and center in a photo of the Hot Half Dozen in 1966, part of a St. Paul Pioneer Press photo feature on local bands titled, "Those Teen Bands!" on June 5, 1966. (Image courtesy Rick Ballot)

eyes bulging out."

And then there was the time the Coronados' bus drag raced the Underbeats' bus down Central Avenue. "I think we were going to win, but I sheered a cotter pin and we lost. I had to bring that bus in every week to be fixed."

After the bus, the band purchased a used ambulance. "But we didn't like to be driving a white ambulance, and so we painted it maroon." It didn't look like an ambulance any more. "We called it, 'the hearse.'"

"We had a couch in there for the guys to sit on in the back, and we'd also put a blanket over the top of our long speakers and somebody could sleep on that. One time, I was trying to back up between some posts, and I couldn't see very well and I ran into one of the posts, hard. Jim was asleep on top of the speakers and he went flying over the corrugated speaker. He said he felt like a piece of cheese that just went through a grater."

Not all the calamities were on the road, sometimes they were on the stage. "One night, for fun, Jim moved over to drums and I played bass. I managed to stay on the beat, but that was my one and only performance on bass.

"Another time, Jim was singing and he called out to Draper, the saxophone player to 'Take it, Fred!' Jim meant he should do a sax solo. Instead, Draper just stopped playing and just started singing. I don't know how we got out of that one."

One of the worst scenes was at a venue in Wisconsin. "They only had one plug-in for the whole band, and it was where the people were walking. We started our opening song, and about four bars in, the power went out. So we went over and plugged in again, and started the song again. After a few bars, we lost the power again.

"We did this about four times, and the band guys were saying we should just move on, but I told them we were going to do this song all night long until we finished it. They tried taping the plug to the outlet and other things, and somehow we got our power back and finished the set."

Ballot's part of the festivities was to be the announcer all night long, a job he enjoyed. "I told a lot of jokes, even though some people thought they weren't very funny. When we did 'Heat Wave' I'd say it was a Martha and the Venereals song. It always got a laugh." By this time, he'd purchased Rogers drums, and had them customized to be the same color as the guitars.

Ballot was also the manager, and every week he'd hand an envelope with that week's pay to each band member. Trouble was, sometimes the expenses outweighed the earnings, and the envelopes were empty. "They'd always say, 'Why give us an empty envelope?' and I'd tell them it was part of my bookkeeping."

Ballot also was responsible for getting whatever vehicle they were using gassed up and ready, and making sandwiches for everyone on the trip. "For the 12 bucks I was paying these guys, I had to supply some food too."

The band got a reputation for always showing up a little late. "We'd leave in plenty of time, but something always happened. We'd have to set up hard and fast. The worst part was tearing down at the end. Everybody was tired."

Despite their success, band members drifted away. New band members were George Knoll and Ron Geslin. They changed the name of the band to the Hot Half Dozen. Ballot doesn't remember if he came up with the name or if it was Ira Heilicher or perhaps Dale Menten. They would practice at Knoll's parents' house in Columbia Heights.

The Hot Half Dozen soon were one of the top bands in the Twin Cities, moving to a more soul sound with horns, rubbing shoulders and sharing billing with the Underbeats, the Chancellors, the Castaways and Gregory Dee and the Avanties. They even had a regional hit, "Heat Wave" with Walsh singing the lead.

Having a hit song was a major breakthrough. "That's all we cared about. We didn't care much about how much money we were going to make from it. But we had this song on this piece of plastic."

Rick Ballot today with the drum cover that was created by his mother back in the 1960s. Did the RB stand for "Rock Band?" He laughs. "No, it stood for Rick Ballot." (Photo by Al Zdon)

The band was playing three times on the weekends, sometimes on polar ends of the state, and sometimes during the week. There was a major ballroom in almost every town in the state, and the Twin Cities had ballrooms and also teen clubs.

"Someone in the band even came up with an advertising idea. They wanted to convince Grain Belt, the major brewery in Minneapolis, to put up a billboard that would say, 'We're the Hot Half Dozen. Try our cold half dozen of Grain Belt.' When Grain Belt found out that none of the members of the band were of drinking age, that idea was flushed."

Not exactly the green room. Walsh changes into his street clothes in a parking ramp after a Coronados' performance.

The Underbeats were considered the best band in Minnesota, and they decided to cut a demo record. They needed a keyboardist and so they asked Walsh to sit in at the studio. A few weeks later, they offered him a job in the band.

"They already had Jim Johnson, Enrico Rosenbaum and Tommy Nystrom doing vocals. And now they added Jim. They had the four best vocalists in the Twin Cities. It was unbelievable."

"Jim tells me he had to struggle with the idea of changing bands, but all I remember was that he dropped his uniform off at 9 in the morning and he was gone."

The Hot Half Dozen continued on, adding new members including Daryl Lichey and Bill Davis. It's both Ballot's and Walsh's opinion that the band actually got better after Walsh left. But trouble was ahead for the band even as they became one of the top groups in the region. Ballot broke his leg and was out several months. When he returned, the band voted on whether to keep the new guy or keep Ballot. It wasn't unanimous, but Ballot got his job back.

Ballot finally decided to pull the plug in 1969. He said his kids were getting older, he was playing softball most nights of the week, and then playing in the band on the weekends was too much. He has rejoined the band for reunions, including when they were named to the Minnesota Rock and Country Hall of Fame.

"It's funny because I was in the band for almost ten years. But the way we broke up – I don't remember much. All of a sudden one day we just weren't there anymore."

Looking back, "I don't miss any of the money we made, what there was of it, but I miss the camaraderie. I miss the guys."

Material came from an interview with Ballot at his home on March 3, 2022, and from an interview he did with Tom Campbell on October 12, 1994.

An early version of the Underbeats with Ray Berg on guitar, Jim Johnson on lead guitar, Rod Eaton on drums and Doni Larson on bass. (Photos courtesy Doni Larson)

CHAPTER FOUR

UNDERBEATS

Everybody young and old
Learn how to rock and roll
Listen, here's something new
Everybody's lookin' to
Foot stompin'
Foot stompin'
Foot stompin'
Foot stompin'
Foot stompin'
Foot stompin'
Foot stompin'
Foot stompin'
Foot stompin'
Foot stompin'
A good time.
—Written by Aaron Collins, 1961
Performed by the Underbeats, 1964-1969

JAMES WALSH:

Back in those days, the Underbeats were the big band. The Avanties were the big band. The Chancellors completed the big three.

We were pretty ragtag as the Coronados, but with the Hot Half Dozen we polished it up quite a bit. I'd like to think I had something to do with that. We kind of got our shit together, changed some players. We were getting better and we started intermingling with these guys

At one point, the Underbeats were doing a recording. So they invited me to come and play on the recording. I was quite honored. They had a keyboard player before, but Jim Johnson said he didn't

In addition to high quality rock and roll, the Underbeats always brought a little class to those early venues. The small decorations on the berets indicated what instrument they played. From left: Rod Eaton, Ray Berg, Jim Johnson, Doni Larson.

like keyboard players because they gave him a headache. So we went to the studio and I played on a couple of songs for them. And that's really where the whole thing started. The Hot Half Dozen played with them at the Prom Ballroom one night, and Jim (Johnson) and Rico (Rosenbaum) and Tom (Nystrom) asked to see me after the show, and they asked me to join the band. Jim was leaving for the service, and they were adding a couple of new band members.

It was very painful for me because it meant leaving my buddies. I'm 17 years old and a junior in high school. Rick Ballot had been my mentor. He was the one who got me involved. Rick took me from the window well to being in a band. It was a painful decision. I was leaving the gang, and joining this other gang of guys, these old guys. They were four or five years older than me.

I can remember to this day sitting at my dad's, out in the driveway, thinking what am I going to do with this? Do I take a step forward or do I take a step back? Do I make it easy, or do I make it hard? I remember lying awake at night in my house, wondering what I should do. I finally decided to make the move, but it took me several days to work up the courage to tell Rick. That was tough. I was the lead singer.

I went down the block to Rick's house. I said, "Something's happened and I got to move forward. This is an opportunity for me." After a little bitching, he got the idea.

FOOT STOMPIN'

So I joined the Underbeats who were the best band in town. Now I've got another set of fucking problems. I've got to learn the songs. So I get the list from Doni Larson, the bass player. It was a long list of rock and roll standards, R&B standards. I just about fell over. He told me I had to know all these songs in three weeks. I remember sitting in the basement and just practicing and practicing, going over the songs. I finally called Doni, and I told him, "I think I'm ready. I think I can do this." I was a nervous wreck.

So we went out to the Safari Club in Mendota Heights. The owner was a good friend of the band, and he let us rehearse there. So I remember going to rehearsal, coming in with my equipment, you know. I had an old Silvertone amp, it had a hole in the top.

We were practicing and Jim said, "You know, your amp sounds funny." I knew what he meant. It was buzzing and it hadn't done that before. I told him I didn't know what it could be, and he said, "Well, let me look in there." He pulled off the back, and there was a piece of pizza in there. A regular nice triangle piece of pizza had fallen through this hole. My amp really sounded really good after that. He said, "Is that better?"

We practiced and practiced, and they assigned me some songs they wanted me to sing. It just kept getting better and better. And like anything you do, I got used to it. But the "every day" was real hard. We would leave for a job every day early and come home late.

Doni Larson with his super-sized bass in 1965.

So now I have a new reality. I'm in the Underbeats. I went from playing a couple of times a week to playing six nights a week. There were ballrooms everywhere in Minnesota. Every night we went out and played. Places like the Bel Rae Ballroom, and there were Bel Rae's all over. It was one of the best times of my life. I was making more money than my dad and I had a new car. It was just crazy nuts.

Jim Johnson was a tough son of a bitch and he always had a plan, and I'm glad that his plan included me eventually. He started the Underbeats, him and Doni Larson, along with Ron Eaton and Ray Berg. Doni was just a neighborhood guy who was not a musician, but Jim got together with him and said, "You're going to play bass in the band." For whatever reason, Doni didn't tell him no. So Jim taught him how to play the bass. They went up to a music store and bought the biggest bass they could find,

Jim Johnson was the founder, lead guitarist and guiding spirit of the Underbeats from the garage to the Whisky A Go Go.

and Doni joined the band.

Jim was a great big Chuck Berry fan. He could sing Chuck Berry, he could play Chuck Berry. He liked that rock and roll sound. He was a good soloist. He could think up some really nice hook lines. What you hear now in Gypsy, we're still using those. He was a good singer. Jim did the low parts, Rico did the middle parts and I did the high parts. We had a nice blend. Rico sang most of the songs, I did the second most, and Jim was third. We always had that harmony, so when we moved to a harmony thing, everybody knew their place. The blend was good in the studio.

We worked on the harmony before Jim left, but we didn't learn about the tricks of the harmony till we got to Los Angeles. Tom Nystrom was in the band, and he also was a great singer. He was in the Accents as their drummer and now he was with us. Tom did the Lonnie Mack song, "Why" for the Accents, and he did it better than Lonnie, better than anybody. He was a big influence on me.

Tom died of cancer a few years ago. He played drums and sang. He was an okay drummer, well actually not a very good drummer. It's too hard for a drummer to do two things that are that important. The drummer is the heartbeat of the band. So I've never liked singing drummers.

Enrico Rosenbaum came from Highland Park. He was Jewish. His parents had met in a concentration camp, and by the grace of God, both were able to get out. They came to America, had Rico, and decided that he would be their only child. He started playing guitar when he was ten or eleven. He came out into the public with a band called the Escapades. They were very popular. They wore Beatle wigs and Beatle boots and did Beatles songs. He was a really good singer. Everybody heard about Rico and his singing.

He was also a good song writer, very prolific with the lyrics. As we look back now, they were somewhat dark lyrics. Aside from his talent, Rico was also a spoiled brat. His mother, Ida, who adored him, spoiled him rotten. So he had this attitude. He always had this attitude of entitlement. With the Underbeats, we had to set our course, and Rico was involved. He was very stubborn about ideas and what we were going to do.

Putting the band together was mainly Jim Johnson's thing. He pulled in Tom on drums, he pulled in Rico on guitar. He pulled me in on keyboards.

But then Jim left. Things over that two-year period changed a little bit. We knew that Jim was coming back. But we knew we wanted to start writing some music, and changing some of the music we were doing. I don't think we were doing any original songs at that time, but we were al-

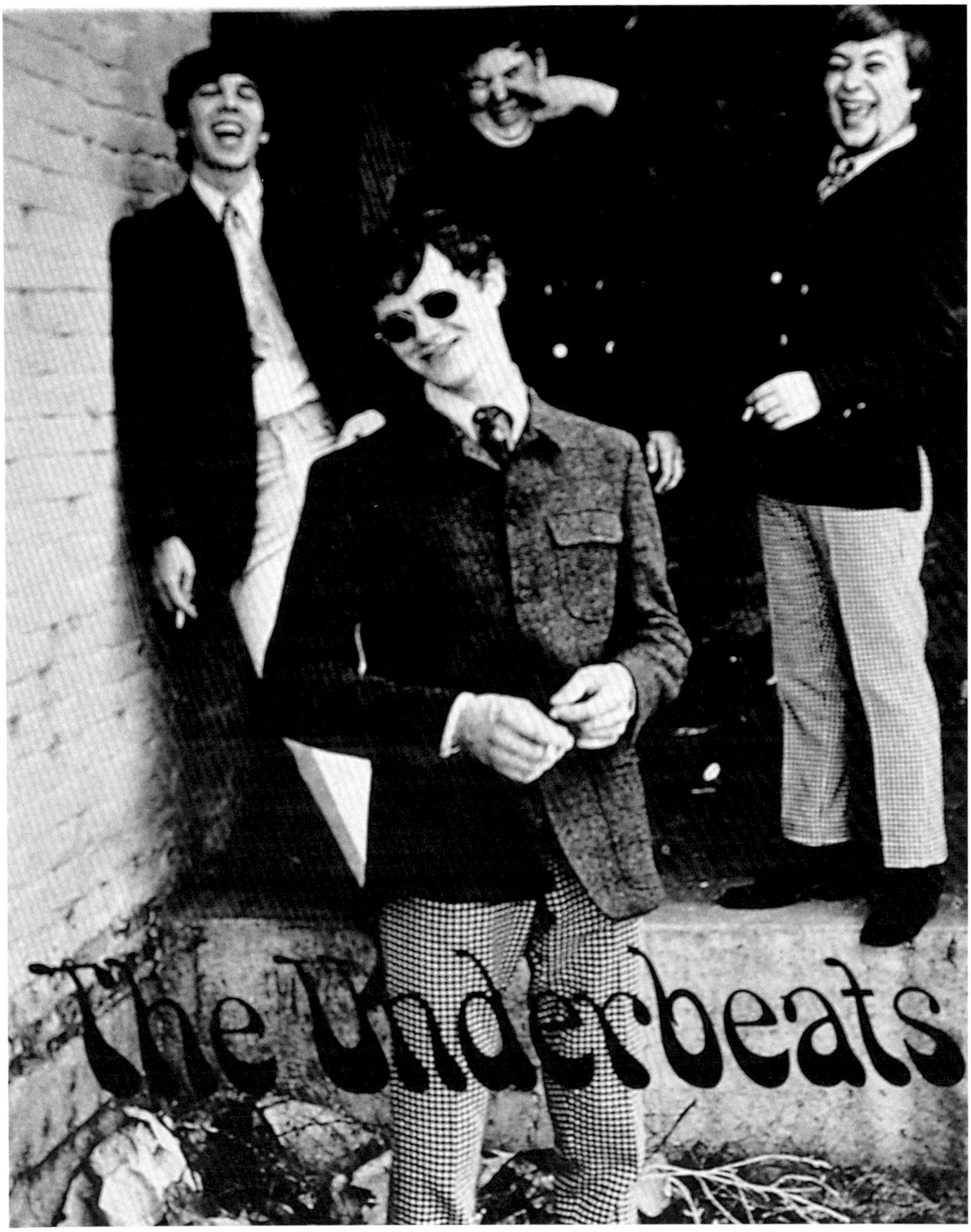

This classic 1966 photo of the Underbeats graced the cover of Rick Shefchik's seminal book about 1960s rock and roll in Minnesota, *Everybody's Heard About the Bird*. James Walsh joined the band not long after this publicity picture was taken. From left in back: Enrico Rosenbaum, Tom Nystrom, Doni Larson. In front: Jim Johnson.

ways trying to do things that nobody else could do, which paid off for us. Nystrom would sing the Supremes stuff, and I had a high voice and would sing these girly songs, and the girls would go nuts about it. We were preparing for Jim to come home. We didn't know that Jim would want to leave so soon when he got back. We thought he'd start playing with us again, and then we'd make the move. But during that time, Rico and I kind of took over the band. Doni took care of the booking. But the vibe changed quite a bit.

Every night, we'd get everything into one van. And every night we'd go out and make money, you know. I was making $150 a week, and that was more than my dad.

School Daze

I wasn't doing anything in school. I wasn't showing up. I tried to cut a deal with the nurse, and she kind of got it. I told her, "I'm playing in Rochester tonight, and I won't get home until three in the morning." She said, "Come in at 10 or 11." So I'd get to school at 10 or 11 and she'd always write me a note. Well one day I told her I had to play that night at Worthington. She said, "Well, you'd better get out of here early."

When I did go to school, I paid one of my friends, Art Burnevik, to get my lunch at noon. Art was one of the better students and was on the student council. It was 35 cents. I'd give him a buck. He'd get my lunch, bring it to my table, and then he'd have a free lunch and a little more. I hated going through that line. That's not called a rock star, that's called a bone-head, out of control, lazy, stupid dude. We always sat at the same table, and so I'd mosey on in there and my lunch would be sitting there. I loved the lunches at Edison. The pizza was great.

One day I went down to Mr. Younghans, the assistant principal, and he already didn't like me. I said, "Mr. Younghans, I have a problem. I can't park my car in the kids' parking lot. It's a new car and they're going to door-ding me and do other stuff." After about a half an hour of talking, he finally said, "Okay, park it in the teacher's lot," and he gave me a sticker. Honest to God.

So I didn't spend a lot of time at school. Even in junior high, there were just teachers that weren't impressed with my effort. I'd get an A in gym and an A in music, and everything else was all Fs. I got my report card at the end of the year and I was walking down the hallway and I looked at my English grade. It was F, F, F, F, and then the final grade was D-plus. I'm looking at it and I'm thinking, this can't be right. So I went to the teacher's room. His name was Mr. Fitzpatrick and everybody called him Porky Pig. He looked just like Porky Pig. And I said, "Mr. Fitzpatrick, I've got to ask you, sir, with all respect. You gave me 4 Fs. And you gave me a D-plus for a final. How does that work?"

And he said, "I never want to see you again."

I said, "Okay, thanks."

In high school it was the same way. I'd show up for this and I'd show up for that. It got bad. I eventually checked out. One morning I got up, and I told my dad we had a chance to go to

Lawrence, Kansas, and play a college club down there called the Red Dog. It was sort of like our Cabooze up here. I said, "The band's going down there and I'm going with them. I'm going to be gone for a couple of weeks. I'm going to check out of school today."

James Walsh in the Edison High School Marching Band from the school's 1966 yearbook called *The Wizard*.

And he said, "Okay." He knew I was distracted already. I was making good money. I had a new car. He didn't have a new car, and I had a new car. I'm 17 now, and I've got a new car.

I went down to the high school and told them what I was doing, and I checked out. I wanted to do it right. I didn't want them to worry. I never went back to get a GED, and that's something I regret. My dad wanted me to do it, but I just wasn't interested in it. It wasn't a big, big deal then. The bug was so firmly implanted inside my brain that music was what I was going to do. I used to play sports, I was a good athlete. I played American Legion baseball and football. I loved sports, I still love sports. I was a great racquet ball player. I could play some tennis. My brother and I were not blessed with a lot of speed, but we could play. My brother played hockey at Mankato State University. We played softball almost every night of the week. I played third base. And then this music thing really took over, and I just veered to the right.

I don't regret it at all. I've made some horrible sacrifices in my life because of music. Good people in my life, several wives… who just wouldn't listen. (laughs) Several really good people. My first two children I was absent a lot. We had to have some meetings about that in later years and I tried to explain to them what I was trying to do. By the grace of God, I accomplished some of what I was trying to do with my career. It wasn't just wasted time on a pipedream. They understood. Everything's good now.

Early on in the Underbeats, I'd come in at 3:30 in the morning and I'd go upstairs where my brother and I shared a room. At about 7 o'clock, he'd come over and say, "Jim, can I use your car?" And I'd say, "Huh?" And so he'd take my car. He did it all the time. My mom would have to give me a ride down there.

So he'd be sitting in class and they'd announce, "John Walsh, bring your brother's keys to the office right away."

Johnson in Vietnam

So Jim went into the service and honored his country. That was a painful goodbye, knowing the possibilities were good that he'd go to Vietnam. Luckily he got to play some music when he was there.

Jim Johnson in uniform.

He would be back in two years, and I would stay in the band. We hired a guitar player named Lauren Walstad from southern Minnesota. He knew going in that this was a two-year gig for him. It was high visibility. At that time we were the number one band in Minneapolis. He was a good guitar player. We had talked about keeping the band's vibe intact. We didn't want to drop its popularity or quality. Everything was carefully planned out.

It was during those two years where we started developing ideas for original music, with the thought that we'd be leaving for Los Angeles. We knew we couldn't land out there with a bunch of crap. Rico and I started developing ideas, and we took over the leadership of the band. Jim had gone in, but he came back home on leave. We had got something going to do some recording. We did a song called "It's Going to Rain Today" that got local radio play.

All these things developed, this three-guy relationship between Jim and I and Rico. It was a good chemistry, it was interesting, and it was vocally acceptable. It worked, we didn't fight. We had three people, and if two voted for something, that was it. We kept that as our standard for how we did our business, and it worked. Of course, mistakes were made. Big mistakes were made.

We started doing a little more recording when Jim was gone. Rico and I started arranging things more, and making the songs our own. We kind of spearheaded the band in Jim's absence. We recorded at Kay Bank Studios just off of Lake Street, and at Sound 80, just a couple of times. All for local radio play. So we started recording, writing a couple of songs, they had me sing lead for the first time. I was nervous. But it all worked out.

On one of those sessions, I can't remember how, but we got involved with David Zimmerman. Someone said he would help us in the studio. It was a good experience, but he didn't help us. He was a good guy, a straight shooter. I can't even remember what songs we did. We really didn't have any good material. Part of being a good producer is to find songs for people, because without songs, it's nothing. You can record 50 shitty songs, and nobody's going to sign you. But if you have one song, "Cuz It's You Girl," then Warren Schatz hears it and shows up two weeks later with a contract. But at that time we had nothing, and nothing we recorded was ever used. But it was a good experience. He was a good guy.

Jim did go to Vietnam but for a time he was lucky enough to play with the USO. I know he did a tour with Martha Raye when she was entertaining the troops. Eventually, though, he wound up in combat. I think it changed him a little bit. He had a couple of encounters that he talked to us about that were life changing. You know, when a person you know dies in front of you in a very terrible way, it leaves a mark. No matter what you think, it leaves a mark.

He came home from the service. We all got together and let Lauren go. I don't know what month Jim got home, but we immediately sat down and Jim said, "We're leaving for California in November. I don't care if you go, but I'm going. I'm not going to stay here and be the big fish in a small pond. I think we have the ability to go out and get a record deal."

We had four really good singers. We had all come from other places and under Jim's tutelage, we had created this Underbeat vibe. Jim and I and Rico were the perfect storm of vocals. The staff was perfect and the timbre was awesome. So we went with that and kind of made it the standard for everything we did. Gypsy was known for its harmony, and that came from the Underbeats.

CALIFORNIA DREAMING

We left that November. We had $500 and two guns and a bus. Along the way, we painted it red, white and blue. Jim painted a Mickey Mouse on the back. It was a hippie bus.

We went to California. Rico was excited about that. We were all excited about that. We had made the commitment to go, we all made sacrifices to go. I had just turned 18 and I had been married in April that year. Rico had his mother and father to deal with, and they didn't want him to go. Jim Johnson had a wife and child who didn't want him to go. But we went.

So now we're on the bus to L.A. We had to be very careful about fuel usage because many of the stations out West had signs that said, "No hippies allowed." And we tried to get gas at one, and the guy absolutely

David Zimmerman is Bob Dylan's younger brother by five years, and he grew up in Hibbing. He managed Skogie and the Flaming Pachucos and other bands in the early 70s, and his company was called Bernard Productions. He produced the Pachucos' first album at Sound 80 Studios, the same studio that was used when Dylan recorded songs for "Blood on the Tracks." David reportedly convinced his brother that the original tracks, recorded in New York, were sub-par. He gathered some Minnesota musicians to complete the album. He lives in Minnesota.

wouldn't let us. He just would not let us buy gas. We were just young people headed out west in 1968, and we couldn't get served.

We arrived in California, and Jim told us we had to rehearse. Just good isn't good enough. We had what was left of the $500, a bus, and not a clue. But we knew where we wanted to be. We had a manager, Steve Freeman, and he had taken over managing the band when we were in Minnesota. We decided to let him take over that role, and help with the financial wherewithal to actually go. Freeman's father owned Freeman Lighting Concepts. They had five or six stores. They had a lot of money and Steve had an XKE. He went out there before us. We had that $500 which we thought was an awfully large amount of money. Of course, now it's a trip to McDonald's with your grand-kids.

Freeman had rented us a home out in the Valley, on Arminta and Arvilada. It had a pool. We lived there and rented a garage and practiced and practiced and practiced. We ate rice and baloney, and then more rice and baloney. That's where the song writing thing began with Jim and I and Rico. I remember it was very infantile in the beginning. We kind of had to mix up the soup before it was done, so we were pretty good at exchanging ideas. It seemed that Rico was coming up with the lyrics, he led the pack. Jim and I were hook lines, or arrangement things. Our first set of songs were terrible. One was called "Dead Babies" or something, and it was stupid.

We starved for a long time. We rehearsed every day. We kept on rehearsing and we kept on re-hearsing. When we didn't have anything to eat, we just practiced every day. Every day. Like Jim Johnson said, and I stick with it today, we can't be good, we've got to be great. And he was right. It was a struggle for a long time. It was hard to find any place to play. We were from Minnesota. They figured we were dumb farmers.

We were still living in the Valley. All the kids around the neighborhood would gravitate to our house because they knew we were musicians. They could hear us practicing in the garage. So we got to know all those kids. The house we were renting was very nice, and it was done in Japanese style, you know, those paper partitions. These kids would be taking downers, and we learned not to let one guy in, George, because he had been taking these drugs and he didn't handle it very well. But somebody let him in, and he just walked through two of those partitions. Just walked right through them.

I needed money bad, and so I sold a guy on acid a gun for $25. I said, "The only thing I want you to do is as soon as I give you the gun, I want you to leave the yard." He gave me the $25 and took off. What was I thinking?

After a couple of months, our manager Steve got us a gig, it was at the Brass Ring out in the Val-ley. We got to be kind of regulars there. It was an older place, but we didn't care. We just wanted to play. Neil Young had played there, and some other people. They were trying to do the same thing that we were.

Steve was beating the path up on the Strip. There was the Troubadour, Gazzarri's, Whisky a Go Go, The Experience. Those were the only four places to play.

Steve finally got Bill Gazzarri to come out and see us. He was the owner of Gazzarri's. The Doors,

Buffalo Springfield, Lolly Vegas, the list goes on and on of the people who played there at Gazzarri's. He said, "Well, I'll give you guys a shot." They had three bands who played there every night, starting at 9 p.m. and ending at 3 a.m. You played twice.

Nobody was as good as we were vocally, and Gazzarri had already kind of caught on to that and started featuring us. The best spot on the bill was the middle place and the last place. And we were always in those slots. Meanwhile, Steve was down the block at the Whisky a Go Go. He talked the doorman, Mario, into asking Elmer Valentine to walk up the street, just a half a block up, to go and see us.

One day, Elmer came up there and he liked the band a lot. He talked to us a little bit. Chicago, known then as the Chicago Transit Authority, was the house band at the Whisky in those days. But their album took off and they were going out on the road. A few weeks later, Elmer called and said, "Chicago's leaving, would you like to take the house band gig here?" Of course, that was a major, major, major, major break for us.

The Underbeats got scale at Whisky a Go Go. The musicians union in the Twin Cities was a joke, but the one in L.A. was very serious. When we went in there, he agreed to pay us scale. That was fine whatever amount of money that was, because he said he'd feed us. Whatever it was, it was probably better than a box of rice and a ring of baloney. By the way, I don't eat baloney and rice anymore.

Feeding us was a very big deal. Every day at 5 o'clock, our hippie bus would roll up there so we could eat. That killed one bird. Then we were the opening act for everybody who came there. It was people like the Kinks, Little Richard, Johnny Rivers, and the list goes on. Eventually he let us be the headliner on weekends.

One day, there was a little earthquake, what they call a shaker out there, and that was enough for Tom Nystrom, the drummer. He just packed up and headed home. We came back to the Twin Cities and auditioned some drummers, and that's where we found Jay Epstein. We brought him back with us.

The Brass Ring was on Ventura Boulevard in Sherman Oaks. In the late 60s it became a well-known venue featuring Eric Burden and the Animals, Delaney and Bonnie, The Flying Burrito Brothers, and the Strawberry Alarm Clock. The location of the club is now a senior living village.

Gazzarri's, a nightclub on the Strip, hit its peak about this time, featuring many of the up and coming bands. Jim Morrison and the Doors, Question Mark and the Mysterians, Bobby Fuller Four, Buffalo Springfield, and the Walker Brothers were some of the bands who played there. Bill Gazzarri, who was born in New York, often dressed up like a Chicago gangster and frequented the club. Gazzarri's was at Doheny and Sunset Boulevard in West Hollywood, adjacent to the Rainbow Bar and Grill and the Roxy Theater. Miss Gazzarri's Dancers, featuring Barbie Benton, strutted their stuff between and during musical acts. Gazzarri's closed after his death in 1991.

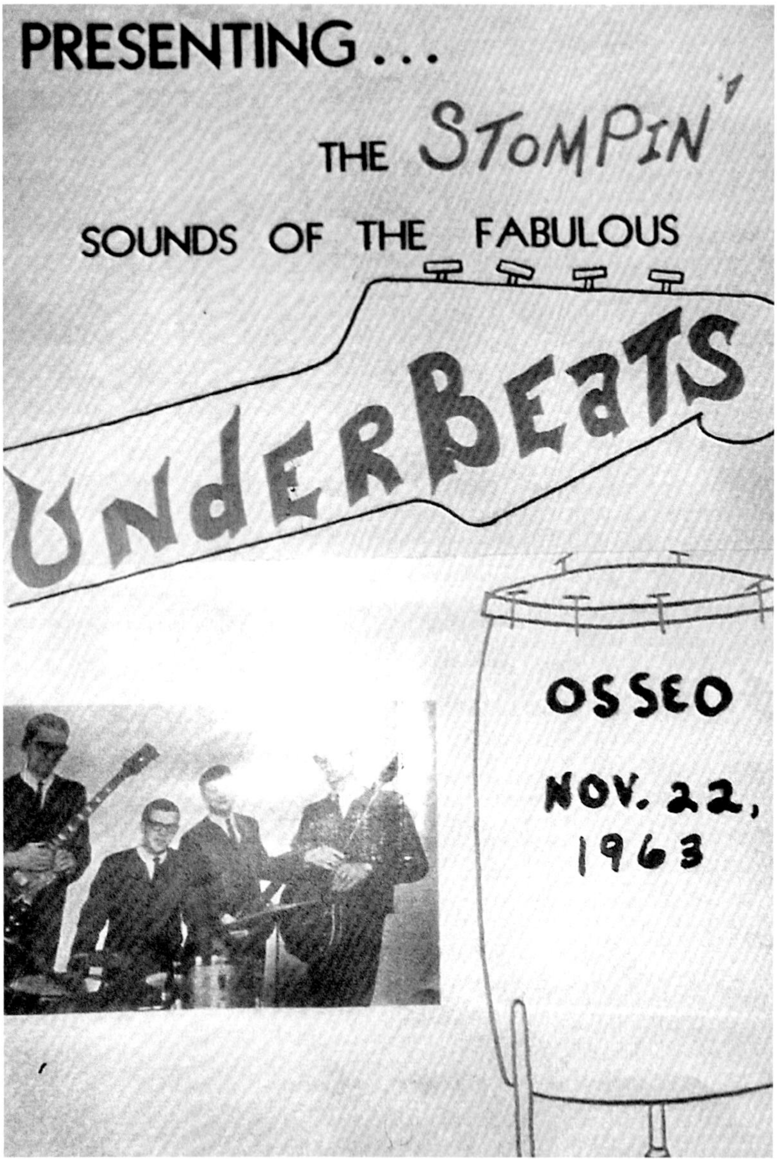

One of the early Underbeats gigs was at Osseo in 1963. The historical significance of the poster is that Nov. 22 is the date that John F. Kennedy was assassinated in Texas. The concert was held as scheduled. (All photos in this section are courtesy Doni Larson)

INTERVIEW

DONI LARSON

By Al Zdon

Doni Larson was there at the beginning.

As a senior at North High School in 1961, he was invited to play bass guitar in a newly formed band. There was only one problem. He didn't know how to play bass, or any other instrument for that matter.

But when the band's first bass player quit because someone threw a snowball and hit his amp, Jim Johnson, the band's leader asked his good friend Larson to fill in. The first step was to buy an electric bass, and so he headed, along with his mother, over to Torp's Music in St. Paul. "We saw this great big Magnatone long seal bass on the wall, and we put down a payment."

"Jim showed me one lick, and that was good enough to play some songs." But Larson went further and took jazz bass lessons in downtown Minneapolis.

"I was never popular in high school because I was working all the time. But I got the bass, and lo and behold, I was pretty good at it." It was the first step toward becoming a rock and roll star.

"We would practice in my mom's basement. We didn't know it, but a group of kids from the neighborhood would gather in the backyard to listen to us." The other band members were Ray Berg on rhythm guitar and Bob DeWayne on drums.

But it was a slow start for the band that would take the name Underbeats. "We practiced for a year and half or two years. Finally some of us threatened to quit if Jim Johnson didn't find us a real job. And then it was me who found our first gig."

That gig was at Bill's Roller Rink in Anoka. It went well.

"Teen nights at ballrooms and other places just exploded around then. Pretty soon we were playing nine gigs, seven days a week. My phone just started ringing off the hook. Everybody wanted us. We could make $100 clear each night, or about $900 a week. I bought a Triumph TR-4 Roadster.

"We never played to an empty house. I know one time we were playing at the Bass Lake Ballroom, and it was so packed, the fire marshal came in and made 30 or 40 kids leave."

Doni Larson leads the rhythm section. The costume of the day was blue jeans and leather vests.

Sometimes playing in some of the venues became somewhat dangerous, with fist fights, drinking and threats. "We bought guns so that we could make sure the equipment was safe after the show. Remember, we were long hairs, we were dirty hippies."

At Rice Lake, Wisconsin, a guy threw an empty whiskey bottle at the band, and then tried to manhandle Larson's wife. "I just knocked him out. We didn't take no crap from nobody."

Another time, also in Rice Lake, the Underbeats were playing and a drunk came by the stage and hit the microphone stand in front of Jim Johnson. The microphone slammed into Johnson's face and split his lip. "Jim put down his guitar in a hurry, and just took off after the guy. I turned to the other guys in the band and said, 'No matter what happens, just keep on playing.' We looked out and the crowd just parted in front of us as Jim went after this guy. And then the crowd moved aside and we could see the guy's feet sticking up in the air. Jim had knocked him right over a railing. Jim walked back to the band, calmly put on his guitar, and finished the song."

And it wasn't just rowdy concert goers that caused the problems, but sometimes it was the venue owners. "We were at Schlief's Little City in Inver Grove Heights. It was owned by Elmer Larson, who was known to screw the bands all the time. There was some kind of incident, a fight with the roadies, and Larson said he wasn't going to pay the band. They thought we were just a rock and roll band, and he could get away with it.

"I came into the room and Jim Johnson had Elmer by the throat up against the wall with his feet dangling. And Elmer was a big guy. Jim let him down, and Elmer said, 'Let me go into the other room and I'll get you your money."

One time at a gig in Mankato, the band got in its bus and was heading home. "The bus for the Hot

Teenagers dance up a storm at the Bel Rae Ballroom in Mounds View in 1966. Band members are, left to right: Enrico Rosenbaum, Jim Johnson, Tom Nystrom and Doni Larson.

Half Dozen was right in front of us. We looked up and the entire band was mooning us."

Larson sometimes got the tough jobs from Johnson. "Jim Johnson decided at one point to fire Rod Eaton, and he gave the job of telling Eaton to me. So I fired him, and the next day he was working with T.C. Atlantic."

The band hired Tom Nystrom, lead singer of the Accents, as their drummer, adding another voice to the mix. "Tom was pretty much a straight-forward drummer. I told him not to worry, I could put the rhythm into it."

The next addition was Rico Rosenbaum. "Ray Berg was married by then and had a kid, and he had a real job." Rosenbaum was with the Escapades, a well-known local Beatles cover band. "Rico was also a lead singer, plus he could play this little two-string rhythm thing."

The needs of the U.S. Army and the Vietnam War broke up many bands in the Twin Cities and the Underbeats were not immune.

"When Jim Johnson was drafted, I did everything I could to try and talk him out of it, but he was determined to go in. He was a patriot." That left a hole in the line-up, and the Underbeats hired two more musicians to fill the gap until Johnson returned. Loren Walstad of Winona was hired as the new lead guitarist. "He was a jazz guitarist and he could play all the notes. He was just a killer guitar player. The first time he played with us he got a standing ovation."

The other newbie was a young kid from Northeast Minneapolis, the lead singer of the band Hot Half Dozen. His name was James Walsh.

"When Jim Johnson came back from the service we all had long hair, and he still had his military cut. He wore a coon skin cap for the first month he was back."

The trip west was not as easy as might be thought. The band was refused gasoline and food at many places because of their long hair. And then at Flagstaff, Arizona, their new bus was pulled over because it was still painted school orange, and that was illegal for a private bus in Arizona.

"So we went down the block and bought some paint and we painted it red, white and blue right there in front of the police station."

In California, the band practiced all day long while their manager, Steve Freeman, tried to find gigs in Los Angeles. One day a fairly strong earthquake rocked the Valley where they lived. "As soon as it was over, there was a knock at the door. It was Tom Nystrom, and he was white as a sheet. He couldn't even talk."

The trembler was too much for Nystrom, and he quit the band and went home. The band went back to Minneapolis for a couple of weeks and auditioned drummers, finally hiring Jay Epstein.

"We had just gotten back to Los Angeles, and we had decided to change the name of the band. We were sitting around a table, and we came up with all these bad names. I finally just said, "We live like a band of gypsies. That was it, that was the name. No more discussion."

By this time, the band was writing a lot of its own music. "Rico would come up with the words and Jim Walsh would put the music to it. I feel bad that Jim never got enough credit for what he did."

The band eventually became a regular at Gazzarri's "a teen spot" that had previously featured Buffalo Springfield and the Doors. While practicing at Gazzarri's one day, the band kept going over one part again and again and again. Finally Rosenbaum's patience wore out and he exploded into a tantrum. "I told him to put down his guitar, that I was going to kick his ass. So I knocked him down. I told him if he misbehaved and embarrassed the band again, I'd do worse. It was one of the incidents that sealed my fate with the band."

Gazzarri's led to other venues and finally to the Whisky a Go Go. And that led to a recording contract and gigs at major concerts. Despite their success, the LA scene was a shock to the band's

With Jim Johnson in the service, the band consisted of Jim Walsh, Loren Walstad, Enrico Rosenbaum, Doni Larson and Tom Nystrom.

Midwestern upbringing. "Outside the Whisky, on the street, you could buy anything you wanted. There was a guy there with a jacket, and he opened one side and it was all watches. He opened the other side, and there were bags of marijuana. And we were just bumpkins who just fell off the turnip truck, and now we were in deep Hollywood."

Playing every night at the Whisky was also a revelation. "We'd say after a set, 'Was that so and so in front?' Yes it was. It might have been Richie Furay, or Jimi Hendrix, or some other star. I think we were ignorant of how lucky we were."

Once the first album came out, the venues got larger and larger. Larson remembers the Atlanta Pop Festival and the stunning opportunity to look out at 300,000 to 500,000 people. "It was about 95 degrees that day and 95 percent humidity. The crowd loved us, and they wouldn't let us leave. We did two or three encores. When we finally left the stage, Walsh went over to the railing and just threw up. I think Rico passed out."

Throughout those years, much of the business of the band fell to Larson. He also got to fix the band's bus and other band member's cars. "They told me I could fix anything."

Though the band was climbing the charts, all was not harmonious between the bandmates. As they grappled with the recording contract and then getting a new manager, Larson was a contrary voice at almost every juncture. "They wanted to be rock and roll stars, but I had two kids, I needed to make money."

Specifically, Larson was convinced that signing with Metromedia rather than Atlantic was a huge mistake, that the company only wanted the band as a tax write-off for all the money Metromedia was making off their only other client, the teen star Bobby Sherman. He also didn't like the road the band was taking with their new manager, who would tie the band to the Guess Who. And privately, he warned band members that Rico's addiction to opiates was a disaster waiting to happen.

He finally quit. "Hey, they replaced me with Willie Weeks. That's not bad. It was a compliment to me." Weeks, who was the bass player for Michael's Mystics in the Twin Cities, went on to become one of the most in-demand session musicians in Los Angeles.

Larson did studio work in Los Angeles for a time, and then moved his family to Marin County for a time before moving back to Minneapolis. He played in bands, taught the bass at B Sharp Music, and worked for the Minneapolis Park Board for many years. He now lives in a two-story cabin on a lake north of Brainerd.

But he remembers those Underbeats and Gypsy years well. "It was the best time of my life. I remember one time, I was in the hallway on the second floor of the Whisky, and there was this guy leaning against the wall. I looked and I looked again. It was Jimi Hendrix. He asked to see Jim Johnson and I took him in. He said he wanted to apologize to the band for stealing their thunder with the name of his new album 'Band of Gypsys.' He was just the sweetest guy you could imagine. Totally down to earth, not like a lot of the rock stars."

Larson said the success of the band was due in part to Jim Johnson's unflappable personality. "He took everything with a grain of salt. One time after we had played at Winterland, Carlos Santana came backstage and asked to see Jim Johnson. Santana said to Johnson, 'I know what's wrong with your band.' Johnson replied, 'Get the fuck out of here,' and he threw him out."

Larson didn't quit playing the bass until a few years ago, when his mentor and friend Jim Johnson died. "It just took the wind out of me. I haven't picked up a bass since."

This interview was done April 19, 2022, at Applebee's in Bloomington.

Doni Larson in 2022.

Jim Johnson in April 1965. (Photos courtesy Jan Rangel)

INTERVIEW

JIM JOHNSON

Jim Johnson died in 2019 at the age of 76. This interview is a compilation, taken from Tom Campbell's interview of the Underbeats for MinniePaulMusic.com in 2010, an interview by Mike Chase on KONZ Radio in Owatonna in 2016, and other sources.

James Calvin Johnson said the first record he ever bought was "Long Tall Sally" by Little Richard. He bought it at a little record store near the White Castle in the Northside Minneapolis neighborhood he grew up in.

The first instrument he played was the trumpet at age 8. "I wanted a guitar, but that wasn't considered a band instrument."

The Underbeats came together in 1962 when Johnson and a friend got together to play some music. "I had met Russell Hagen from Columbia Heights. He built cars and hot rods. For some reason we got together and played guitars one day, and we knew this was it. We were going to quit school."

Soon after, though, Hagen decided to join the Army. "We were going in on the buddy system. But I talked with my parents about it, and they said, 'That might be a bad idea, Jimmy.' "

Picking a name for the band was a debate. "We wanted something with 'Beats' in it and we came up with Downbeats, Backbeats and some others. Finally someone suggested Underbeats. We said, 'Yeah, that's it,' but what the hell is an underbeat? We went with it anyway, it didn't have to make sense."

The Underbeats first gig was at the Anoka Roller Rink, where they played with their little basement amps. "But we killed it. I can't remember what we played except I'm sure there was a lot of Chuck Berry."

There was frustration before that first gig in the band because all they did was rehearse. "I kept saying we can't be okay, we have to be excellent. We hit the ground running. We rehearsed all the time, sometimes even when we were playing. We just rehearsed all the time."

After Hagen left for the service, Johnson took over most of the vocals. "I was stuck with it."

The band did songs by the Everly Brothers, Bo Diddly, Buddy Holly, Berry and other hit makers of the era. They deliberately chose songs other bands wouldn't touch. "Most of what we did were songs nobody else played. We wanted to give these songs another chance. But then other bands started playing them. That kind of pissed me off.

"But we had what nobody else had. We were the only band in town doing harmonies."

From about 1963 to 1965, the band worked all the time, sometimes playing nine gigs a week. They were forced to turn down jobs because they had no room in their schedule.

The band's first concert was at a football field in LaCrosse, after participating in a parade.

Somewhere in there, the band also began carrying guns because there were problems loading the gear after some gigs. Drunken customers would interfere. "We had to get the guns out a few times just to get the gear out."

And they wore matching suits. "We went to a store downtown and had the suits specially made. They had a Nehru top and Army green pants with black piping. And we had Italian boots." And for a time, the band all wore matching berets with little musical symbols on them. "I think I saw a picture of Chuck Berry in a beret and I thought it would be pretty cool to do that."

Most gigs were the same. "It would take us an hour to set up, an hour to play, and an hour to get the hell out of there."

The band recorded at several studios and had a regional hit with "Foot Stompin'," which had been a hit for a Los Angeles doo-wop group called the Flares. Once when playing the song at Danceland, an Excelsior ballroom, the floor began to collapse from the dancers participating in "Foot Stompin."

George Garrett recorded the Underbeats' songs and put them out on three labels including Garrett, Bangar and Twin Town. "We'd get the record and go right down to WDGY and they'd play it."

Johnson said the top bands in 1964 were the Underbeats, the Avanties, the Trashmen and the Accents.

One of the releases on the Bangar label was "Little Romance" but the radio stations wouldn't play it. "It had a 'thump thump' where some words would have gone, and the stations thought it was too sexually suggestive so they wouldn't play it."

Tom Nystrom of the Accents joined the band in 1965, replacing Rod Eaton, and Enrico Rosenbaum of the Escapades replaced Ray Berg in 1966. Nystrom was a drummer, but had a terrific high voice. He sang lead on the Accents hit "Why."

"When I heard the Escapades, I had to have Rico. I got him out of there right away. This guy was just the killer in town. The women loved him. He had a great attitude. He was just a very talented guy."

When the Beatles came to Met Stadium in 1965, the Underbeats were one of several local bands that played in the concourses prior to the Beatles show. "We played in the hallway, and I'm still not very proud of that. To me it was embarrassing. I mean, really, playing in the hallways?"

"When the Beatles came on, we tried to listen to them, but with the girls screaming, it was impossible. I do remember that they were pretty hoarse. They didn't sound very good."

Johnson says he never saw Chuck Berry, his musical idol, play live. "I did try to call him one time, and I got close. Finally one of his people just said, 'You don't want to talk to Chuck.' "

The band would earn from $150 to $175 per night, and maybe earn $200 or more for a private party.

Johnson went in the Army in 1966. "We looked for a guitar player who could sing lead, but there weren't any. We were rehearsing at the Ritz Theater in Northeast one time when Wally Walstead from Willmar sat in. "This guy could be somebody, I thought. He could play all those jazz notes. But now we still needed another singer, and James Walsh (from the Hot Half Dozen) was excellent. He could sing his butt off. Plus we could add keyboards to the band. In those days the organs would give me a headache. It was the Farfisas and those Hammond guys who would just lay on that one note forever. But Jim was a decent organ player."

"I really didn't plan on going to Vietnam and being in the infantry. I served in the 4th Infantry Division. When I got to Vietnam, I still had my Fender Telecaster in my duffle bag. A guy asked if I was a professional player, and I said I was. He said he'd send a letter to Saigon to see if I could get in an Army band. I was out in a forward position for three months when a letter arrived, saying I had an audition in Saigon."

He was the guitarist for Martha Raye's USO troupe in 1968 when the Tet Offensive occurred. "We played in forward bunkers all over Vietnam, where other USO tours would never go. Maggie (Martha Raye) was quite a gal."

In 1968, Johnson's tour ended. "I'm sure those two new band members never thought I was going to come home. But I surprised everybody. I made it."

"When I got back, we didn't need a guitar player, and so Wally left. But this Walsh, I liked his voice and the way he played seemed to fit in. So we kept Walsh."

Johnson said his position in the band changed after he got back from the service. "It was very different. I was no longer the leader. Rico and Steve Freeman, our manager, took over that role. I was just tickled to be alive and I lost a lot of my leader qualities. I was just happy to be there, and go along with the program."

Yet, he led the move to California. "I'd been thinking about California for five years. I was going there one way or another. Plus I was used to Novembers without snow." The band left about Thanksgiving in 1968.

Johnson said the Minnesotans were just country bumpkins in Los Angeles when they got there. "I remember we were in the bus and I looked down at a car and there was Beaver's mother (from the hit family show, "Leave it to Beaver.") We were just star-struck. It was Beaver's mother."

The band got regular work, after a long period of rehearsals, at Gazzari's and then at the Whisky A Go Go. "We were unlike anybody else who was playing out there. We had four lead singers and perfect harmony. We were awkwardly unique, but we did it for a reason. We were definitely different, and that made us popular."

The band changed its name to Gypsy, and soon had a recording contract. "We were only the second group, after Chicago, to have a double album as our first album. I don't know how we got away with that, but nobody could control us. We were famous for not being controlled."

After the breakup of Gypsy, Johnson continued to live and play and write music in Los Angeles. Both Ray Charles and Guitar Shorty recorded his song, "Too Hard to Love You." And Johnson wrote two songs, "Magic in My Life" and "Don't Stop for Nothing," for the Fifth Dimension's "Earthbound" album. "Magic in My Life" was released as a single. He played for years in California and later back in Minnesota as Calvin James, a flip-flop of his first two names.

Johnson was the inaugural recipient of the Bill Diehl Music Award in 2016 for a lifetime achievement in rock and roll.

Jim Johnson played and recorded in the 1990s as Calvin James.

An early poster for the Whisky A Go Go in Los Angeles, probably late summer of 1970. Gypsy was slated to open for John Mayall one of England's legendary blues and rock musicians.

CHAPTER FIVE

GYPSY AT THE WHISKY

I hope you'll take heed
And prepare for all I've said
You've had fair warnin'
Gypsy Queen lies ahead
Enrico Rosenbaum
Gypsy Queen, Part 1, 1970

JAMES WALSH:

A couple of weeks after we started at the Whisky and we were still the Underbeats, a fellow named Leonard Feather came by. He was the number one music critic in L.A., and he hung around there a lot. We didn't know this.

He wrote a beautiful article in the *Los Angeles Times* that was just a glowing review of the band. He said these guys from Minneapolis can really sing. They have good musicianship. He said the only trouble was their name. It was really outdated. So we got together and decided to change the name. So we discussed several really bad names.

One night we just decided this was the night. We were going to change the name that night. So we sat around the campfire and we smoked some pot. And then we smoked some more pot, and then we smoked some more pot. We were throwing out these names, horrible names. I can't even remember what they were.

Out of the blue, Doni Larson, the bass player, said, "You know we live just like a band of gypsies." We all said, "Gypsy, that's it. That's it." And that's how we changed the name. So we went back and told Elmer at the Whisky that we had changed the name. He said, "Well, I don't give a shit." And that's how we became Gypsy.

So Gypsy was the house band at the Whisky for about a year or more. That was the place to be

Leonard Feather, London-born, musician and jazz critic, wrote the *Encyclopedia of Jazz.* He was a music columnist for the L.A. Times and a noted composer in his own right. His positive review of the Underbeats performing at the Whisky, and his suggestion that the group could use a new name, both were important to the rising band.
Along the way, Feather did arrangements for Count Basie and produced debut recordings of Sarah Vaughan, George Shearing and Dinah Washington. He wrote reviews in Esquire, Playboy, and Downbeat magazines. Feather won the first journalism Grammy ever in 1964. He died in 2014. (Photo from the University of Idaho)

every night. They were open until two or three. At the end of the night, everybody was there. The Doors were there, Fleetwood Mac, the list goes on. That was the celebrity place to be.

So one night, Bobby Sherman came in. He had a TV show and a hit song. He listened to us, and he went back to Metromedia and talked to Artie and Tommy Valando, the Valando brothers, who were in charge of Metromedia Records. Metromedia was this huge conglomerate, but they had dabbled into this record thing with Bobby Sherman. He told the Valandos, you've got to go up and see these guys, they're really good. So they came up there, and they loved the band. Steve, our manager, was negotiating on possibly doing a record deal with them.

In the meantime, at Atlantic Records, Ahmet Ertegun heard about the band and showed up at the Whiskey one night and he also loved the band. He asked, "Can you guys come down and rehearse next Thursday so I can hear you with no one else around?" We said, "Of course we will."

Ertegun was king of the world. He came to hear us play at the Whisky in the afternoon in a black Rolls-Royce limousine and he had about 10 people with him. We played for him, and they liked it. They made us an offer, and we blew it. I think our music could have been more, but we were afraid of being lost in the shuffle at Atlantic and we thought the other thing, being a band with a label that had no other bands, was more appealing. We signed with Metromedia.

Do you know what the odds were of little Jimmy Walsh from 3459 Northeast Pierce Street getting in a bus and going to Los Angeles and getting a record deal in 1970? It was a jackpot you couldn't win. But we were dedicated to one another, and we had to at least try. And it was tough. And we were tough. It was Northeast and it was North Side. Jimmy Johnson and Doni Larson were tough guys. I wasn't a tough guy, but I was a Northeast guy which automatically gives you some built in toughness. Rico wasn't so tough, but we just went out there with this thing in our hearts.

So, we went from a ring of baloney and rice playing in the garage, to Gazzarri's where we could get hamburgers, to the Whisky who would feed us. We had other things on our mind at that time. I know now that the Whisky was the place, and it still is today one of the hottest places in the United States for rock and roll bands.

Women? Women. Playing at the Whisky was like fishing in a well-stocked trout pond. I was young. I was thin. It was sensational.

One of the bonuses of the Whisky is that all these stars would come through in the upstairs dressing rooms, it was unbelievable. We're back down in the barrel looking up. Little Richard came by. The Kinks came there for the first time. We got to play in front of them. The upstairs at the Whiskey, it's like a building on Central Avenue in Northeast, they had apartments. Those were the dressing rooms. They had an office up there.

So I'm sitting on the stairs one night at the Whisky. I was just sitting there by myself, drinking a bottle of Lancer wine. These two guys come by me. And, I thought to myself, "What the fuck, that was Jimi Hendrix and Buddy Miles." So I go shooting up the stairs. Hendrix went into the can, so I follow him into the can, and I'm standing there like a Minnesota farmer, watching him piss. I realized what I'm doing, and I went into the dressing room. In a little bit, Hendrix came into the dressing room. He said, "Well I just wanted to come down and apologize for using your name Gypsy on the Band of Gypsies album." We said we didn't give a shit, we'll probably sell more albums because of it.

So he and Buddy Miles were there and we were smoking massive quantities of pot and hash. Buddy Miles was a big guy and he took a huge hit of the hash. I'll never forget that hit, it would have put out a small fire. So at the end of the night we invited Jimi Hendrix to come up to our house. Now we're living in Laurel Canyon. We've moved from the Valley into Laurel Canyon. It was closer to the Whisky. My neighbors were Frank Zappa, who lived right on the corner, and then you went up the hill, past our place, and the next place was Mickey Dolenz of the Monkees.

Hendrix came up there and he spent three days with us. We got out massive quantities of cocaine and pot

Bobby Sherman grew up in California, and was discovered by Sal Mineo. He signed with an agent in 1964 and later became a regular cast member on *Shindig!* Starting in 1968, he also was a cast member on *Here Come the Brides*. He received more fan mail than any other performer on ABC.
He did 10 albums up to 1976 and had seven gold singles and five gold albums. In 1969, he signed with Metromedia and had an immediate hit with "Little Woman," selling over one million copies. While he continued to perform now and then, he basically gave up his show business career in 1974 when he trained to be an emergency medical technician. He was once giving aid to a woman who had passed out, and her husband finally said, "Look, honey, it's Bobby Sherman." The woman opened her eyes, stared at Sherman, and said, "Oh, I must look a mess." He signed an autograph for her.

Ahmet Ertegun was born in Turkey and moved to the U.S. at age 12 when his father was the Turkish ambassador to the U.S. He and others formed Atlantic Records in 1947 and had a string of hit albums in the 1950s including Big Joe Turner, the Clovers, the Drifters, the Coasters and Ray Charles. In the 60s, Ertegun and Atlantic developed the growth of soul music with such artists as Otis Redding, Ben E. King and Aretha Franklin. Ertegun then moved on to rock and roll with the Rascals, Led Zeppelin, and Crosby Stills and Nash. When he auditioned Gypsy in 1970, he had sold Atlantic, but was still in charge of finding and producing new talent. At about the same time he made an offer to Gypsy, he signed the Rolling Stones to Atlantic. He is a founder of the Rock and Roll Hall of Fame, and later was inducted. He died in 2006 when he tripped and struck his head at a Rolling Stones concert.

and hash, and he just stayed over. It was like a sleepover. We played a little bit, but not too much. The problem was that he didn't have a left-handed guitar with him. He fiddled around with Jim's but it wasn't right for him. But it was a wonderful three days. Jim and Jimi were war buddies, they'd both been in the service. So they hit it off right away. It was really cool.

During the time we were doing the second album at Larrabee Sound Studios on Larrabee, a girl comes in one night and she sat down. She stayed for quite a while, and we smoked a bunch of pot and we were recording the songs. She said, "I'm going to leave now," and she looked at me and said, "Would you walk me to my car?"

So, of course, Mr. Minnesota Nice said, "Sure I would." I walked her out and she had a white Rolls Royce, right hand drive. I opened the door for her, and she turned around started kissing me and hugging me and said, "How'd you like to come up to my place?" I said, "I'm kind of busy here." She said, "Well, we always have parties up there." And I said, "I can't right now." So she left. It was Cass Elliot, Mama Cass. She lived in the house where everybody lived, Stephen Stills, Jackson Browne, all those guys that were hanging around with the Mama and the Papas. They all lived in this house up in Laurel Canyon. That was another of the great mistakes along the way. I should have gone with her and taken one for the band. Or taken one for myself, because none of those people were that popular then either. They were more popular than we were. I should have gone with her that night. But I didn't.

As things got better, we moved out to Los Feliz and bought a duplex out there, side by side. It was next door to the LaBiancas. You could sit in our dining room and overlook Burbank and see all the way to the ocean. It was fantastic. Everything was Spanish motif, arches everywhere. We lived there for quite a while when we worked at the Whisky.

The morning after the LaBiancas were murdered by the Manson Family, the police busted our doors down. They were canvassing the whole area, and I'm sure they heard that there were a bunch of hippies living next door. They came storm trooping into our house, breaking

Gypsy at the time of their first album. In front, Rico Rosenbaum and Jay Epstein. In back, James Walsh, Doni Larson, Jim Johnson. (Photo courtesy Jay Epstein).

LaBiancas

On August 10, 1969, the city of Los Angeles was reeling from a violent murder of movie star Sharon Tate, Hair Stylist Jay Sebring and three others. Four members of the Manson Family participated. The victims were stabbed and shot in grisly fashion. The next night, Manson accompanied his followers and told them to drive to 3301 Waverly, a house that was next door to a house they had attended a party at the year before. The home was occupied by Leon and Rosemary LaBianca. Leon was a supermarket executive. Manson left, but his clan murdered the LaBiancas by stabbing them multiple times. Words were written on the walls and refrigerator in the victims' blood. The four murderers and Manson were all convicted and given the death sentence, which was later commuted by California law to life imprisonment. The murders, some said, marked the end of the hippie counterculture, probably a gross overstatement. Vincent Bugliosi, a Los Angeles District Attorney who grew up, like Bob Dylan, in Hibbing, Minnesota, wrote a book on the crimes called *Helter Skelter*, which remains the top-selling true crime story ever published.

down the door. They separated everyone. They wanted to know where everyone was that night, what we did. Luckily we were playing at the Whisky, so that kind of got us off the hook, but the murders happened late at night.

So I'm asleep in my room, naked, hair down to my waist, and this guy comes into my room and he says, "Get out of bed, hippie." He's pointing a gun at me. I had an American flag as my bedspread, he pulled it right off.

So, of course, we probably had some illegal stuff lying around. Illegal stuff? We had a pot field in the back yard. It was fucking righteous. One of the detectives went back and looked at it, and said, "What are you kids going to do with that pot?" We said, "Well, hopefully, we were going to smoke it." Plus, we had shit lying all over the house, but they weren't interested in that.

That was a couple of weeks of hassle. We had to get the door fixed, and they kept coming back. They interrogated us again, but we had a pretty good excuse. We were all there at the same time.

But we were part of history.

Rise to almost stardom

I still don't get it. I still don't get it. It's kind of sad. I probably could have gotten more out of it, the whole experience, had I known better, if I was smarter. I was a kid following the wave. One wave would come, and then the next one would come, and then the next one. I smoked my way through that whole fucking thing, which probably was a mistake. And then we started taking acid.

We took acid one time, me and Timmy, Rico, a couple other people, and we played Monopoly for 14 hours. We lost all track of time and that was very strange. Another time, when we were back in the Twin Cities, I took acid and went to the Uptown Theater with Bill Lordan. He said he wanted to take acid and go watch that Disney movie, Fantasia. We sat through that twice without knowing it. When we got back in the car, Bill turned to me and said, "Which part of that did you like the best, the first part or the second part?" Each viewing was a totally different experience.

Our manager had a white XKE. We would take acid at night, me and Timmy (McCarthy, the road manager), and maybe one other guy, Jay or Rico. Steve knew we were on acid but he'd say, "Here take my car and drive out on the freeway. So I would drive the car, and Rico was in the passenger seat, and Timmy was sitting on the little console between the seats. He was sitting higher so his head would be above the windshield.

We were going 100 miles an hour. I looked over at him and his eyes were just so large. We were higher than a kite on acid. That was our recreation when we first got there. We couldn't afford anything else to do.

Then there was the Strawberry Alarm Clock incident. That was a strange one. We were at the Whisky, and they had played there, and they were looking for a keyboard player. They already had "Incense and Peppermints" out. So they called me and I went up to their house, I think it was in Laurel Canyon somewhere, and just played with them for a while. They called me back to hire me, but I told them I'd decided not to do it. Probably should have done it, and I probably should have gone home with Mama Cass too. So many mistakes.

The core of Gypsy was Jim and I and Rico. It's like the Bee Gees, they could have anybody playing with them, as long as those three guys were there. That was a great band for a while. Willie Weeks went off and did something better, which we couldn't blame him for. Bill Lordan stayed with us for three albums, then he left.

Strawberry Alarm Clock was a psychedelic rock band from Glendale, California, a suburb of Los Angeles. Like most groups, they evolved from several bands in the area, and early on made an album, only to have the master tapes stolen. Their first hit, "Incense and Peppermints," was released in 1967 and reached number one on the Billboard chart. The album that followed reached number 11 on the charts. At one point, they had roadies carry them on the stage to open their act on "magic carpets."
Several of their shows in the South were canceled after the assassination of Martin Luther King in 1968, and several of the band members began carrying guns when touring in the south, including on stage. During the time they considered hiring Walsh as a keyboardist, the band was going through constant personnel changes. The band broke up in 1971, but has had several re-incarnations since and they performed at the Whisky a Go Go in 2021.

INTERVIEW

JAY EPSTEIN

Jay Epstein started playing the drums when he was in grade school in Winona, Minnesota, and his first love was jazz. Now in his 70s, he still performs with a dozen different groups around the Twin Cities, and in his heart, it's still jazz.

"When I was a kid, I got into Bennie Goodman and all the swing bands. I loved the progressive sound. I was drawn to the music totally – Count Basie, Miles Davis, Oscar Peterson, Bill Evans, Coltrane."

Epstein played in high school and college doing river boat shows, Dixieland, and jazz. By the mid-60s, Epstein was still a jazz player, but he started to play in some rock ensembles. In 1968, he was in the New World Congregation, a Winona band that released a single. They once played as the warm-up band to Twin City rockers T.C. Atlantic.

In 1969, the premier Minneapolis rock group, the Underbeats, had moved to L.A. to seek their fame and fortune, but a few months later, their drummer, Tom Nystrom, after experiencing a California trembler, decided to come home. The band came back to Minneapolis to audition drummers.

"I thought, 'The Underbeats, these guys are good.' I'd been impressed by their music. I got in contact with Steve Freeman, their manager. We auditioned at Pudge's Club in Highland Park. I got to meet the guys and we played for an hour or so. I know I was playing on Nystrom's drum set.

"They liked me, and I liked what they were doing. You could tell these guys were really together. They offered me the job. I was pretty thrilled."

Epstein still had six months to go at Winona State to get his degree, but

Jay Epstein, Gypsy drummer, poses outside the Whisky A Go Go in front of a larger than life poster of himself. (Photos courtesy Jay Epstein)

he put down his books and headed for California. "I was all for it. I loved it. The guys were so dedicated and professional. I was between school, a girl friend, and music, but the allure of the Underbeats drew me. I liked their commitment of going at it 24 hours a day. I welcomed that challenge."

Epstein sent his drums ahead on the Underbeats' red, white and blue bus, and then drove his Triumph TR3 sports car to Los Angeles. "I loved that car, I had it for 50 years. When I got out to Los Angeles, I found out Rico (Rosenbaum) had a Mercedes Benz, and Freeman had a Jaguar XKE.

After Jay Epstein joined the group at the beginning of 1970, they posed for a photo at Magoos in Minneapolis. From left: Jim Johnson, Doni Larson, Jay Epstein, Tim McCarthy (road manager), Jim Walsh and Enrico Rosenbaum. Larson is giving the photographer the traditional North Side salute.

That's when I knew I was in the right place. I only wish I'd taken a picture of us with our cars."

The band was living in Los Feliz. "I could see the LaBianca's house from my window."

"We were mainly playing clubs out in the Valley, and one of them was the Brass Ring. I know we did a road trip to Colorado Springs one time. And then we moved up to Gazzarri's on Sunset Strip. The next stop was the Whisky a Go Go."

The Underbeats became Gypsy about that time. "We were still doing mainly covers, but we were building up our repertoire for more serious stuff. It was a pretty democratic situation. It was nicely democratic. Someone would bring in a tune, but they'd never say how to do it. We all had an equal voice, you know, whatever feels good to you. We bounced ideas off each other quite a lot. The band had a main musical direction, but we were all relatively equal in shaping the material. Of course, not all the ideas would work.

"We rehearsed around the dining room table most days of the week. We would just work and work on the material, honing the tunes. I loved their work ethic. It was good for all of us. It was deadly serious stuff. I loved being immersed in it, the depth of that kind of professionalism."

Epstein was writing poetry at the time, and he showed his work to Rosenbaum, the band's main songwriter. "Rico was pretty interested in my writing, and I'm glad he was." The result was a co-credit on the first album, "Dream if You Can," by Rosenbaum and Epstein.

Epstein gave Freeman the manager a lot of credit for hustling gigs for the band as they got their feet wet in the West Coast scene. "He was friendly with the girl doing the booking at the Whisky, let's just say they were close friends. All of a sudden we were offered the house band job at the Whisky. You could call that a coincidence."

Being the house band meant three to five gigs a week and often being the opening act for other bands: King Crimson, the Kinks, Little Richard, Albert Collins, B.B. King.

The Gypsy bus was attacked by an unknown Tyrannosaurus Rex.

Band members Jay Epstein and Enrico Rosenbaum happened to be at the Whisky A Go Go when a worker was changing the large sign out front. They convinced the worker to put up the "Featuring Jay" and later "Featuring Rico" on the sign for picture purposes. It was later taken down. Note the large photos of the band members at street level.

"I don't know if we ever played with Chicago, but all the bands had softball teams, and we played them one time."

As time went on, Gypsy would often headline at the club. There were also plenty of concert gigs around town. "I know we went up to Monterrey and we were billed with Arthur Lee and Love and the Chambers Brothers."

Freeman arranged a demo session where Gypsy recorded "Cinnamon Girl," the Neil Young song, and shopped it around trying to attract a recording contract.

After one performance at the Whisky, Rosenbaum and Epstein were asked by the Young Rascals' guitar player Gene Cornish to come to where his band was staying at the Beverly Hills Hotel. They talked about producing Gypsy. "For some reason, that never happened."

The band finally agreed to go with Metromedia. "They produced the album, but they didn't put any money behind it once it was recorded." Epstein recalled how corrupt much of the music industry was in those days with payola often buying radio time. "I think about $5,000 could have greased the wheels of progress for Gypsy."

He also remembers that the band was not paid well for the recording session, but it was a great session. "We had great vocals, and the original material was inventive and appealing."

The band began some serious touring including the Fillmore West in San Francisco where they were billed with Poco and Spirit. They played with Delaney and Bonnie (including Eric Clapton) at the Shrine Auditorium in L.A., and with Doctor John in Detroit.

Epstein is straightforward about the reason he left the band. "They kicked me out." Looking back, "I think the improvisational side of my playing was coming out too strongly. After that, the guys were disappointed in my playing."

He says you can hear what he brought to the band in the first album. "I brought a lot of jazz and improvisation, and at the time that was valuable to them. Later on, it wasn't valuable."

Epstein returned home in December 1970 and finished his studies at Winona State, earning degrees in math and chemistry. But jazz drumming was his profession of choice and he never used his academic accomplishment to make a living. Instead, he played in bands in Minneapolis, Montana, Miami and Oklahoma City, where he played in a bar owned by the Mafia. For five years he played in bands on cruise ships, living on the ships. He's done seven or eight European tours with jazz bands.

Gypsy's road crew — Timmy McCarthy and Kenny — take a break. McCarthy, among other chores, drove the bus, set up the drums, and secured the bands' rooms on the road. When Gypsy disbanded, he worked for several other notable bands.

And now he still plays about 20 gigs a month, contributing to about 15 bands around the Twin Cities.

Looking back, he has strong memories of Gypsy, especially the three lead singers, Jim Johnson, Enrico Rosenbaum, and James Walsh.

"Rico was so acerbic. You might say he was an egotistical asshole. But he was a tremendous lead singer. He was filled with magnetism. I loved the guy, except when I didn't. It was unforgivable what he did to his mother.

"But as an artist, he was mesmerizing, bigger than life.

"I wasn't surprised when he died. He was into that cocaine world, plus I think he was devastated that the band didn't have more success. He deserved much wider success and acclaim for what he was. He should have been a super star."

Rico Rosenbaum in about 1970

"We called Jim Johnson 'Soul Dad.' He was the eldest cat in the band, and he had a really solid, wonderful musical sense. I had a lot of respect for Jim, partly because of his attitude about playing and also for his work ethic.

"Jim was what in jazz bands we would call a 'woodshed musician,' he was always trying to improve his playing, his technique. I think we were musically kindred souls, always trying to express ourselves in a musically pure way."

"Owl is just an effervescent, joyful spirit and that comes across in his music. I like that. He has a positivity that's attractive. You want to be part of that. When we were in Los Angeles we would get into the longest, greatest laughing sessions. They would go on for hours. He just has that joie de vivre, and I still love him. We're still the Flying Acid Brothers."

Six decades into his career with the drumsticks, Epstein is content where he's at and where his music is at. "I don't care if I'm playing before 10 people, 50 people or 3,000 people. I'm somewhat oblivious to the crowd or their response. Maybe because I've played in so many jazz bars where these shitty conversations are going on while you're trying to play.

"It's not why I'm there. I'm there to play the best music I can and contribute to the musicality of the band to the best of my ability.

"The audience, well, I'm glad they're digging it."

Jay Epstein in 2022.

This interview was done by Al Zdon and Jay Epstein in Bloomington, Minnesota, in 2022.

GYPSY

CHAPTER SIX

RECORDING

It's a long, long road
From which there is no return
While we're on the way to there
Why not share?
He Ain't Heavy, He's My Brother
Bob Russell, Bobby Scott, 1969

JAMES WALSH:

We started writing better songs. I think the reality of knowing that we had a record deal got our enthusiasm up. So we're writing songs, and we're writing good songs.

For instance, "Dead and Gone." Rico would come with the beginning, and then Jim and I would enhance the end, plus all the little ups and downs. So, the chemistry was perfect. We were writing away. They had given us a budget. And then one day, after we had smoked a lot of pot, we decided, "Well, we've really got a lot of songs. We should do a double album like Chicago." Chicago was the first rock group to debut with a double album, and ours was the second one.

So we head up to Hollywood to see the Valando brothers, and we're sitting around the desk and these two guys are looking at us. "We want to do a double album." They told us, "You guys are crazy, you're absolutely crazy." So we talked them into a double album. It cost them $37,000. They told us we were absolutely nuts.

News gets around fast when you have a contract. People started approaching us because they had heard we had a two-record deal and they had songs. We had some great songs, but we had all these stupid songs, like "Dead Baby." I didn't write them, Rico was the writer. I don't know when he got

Bobby Scott (Wikipedia)

"He Ain't heavy, He's My Brother" was written by Bobby Scott and Bob Russell. At the time Russell was dying of cancer and they only met three times to collaborate, but they managed to write it. When Gypsy turned the song down, it was shopped to producer and singer Kelly Gordon, but the song failed to chart. It was later recorded by the Hollies, where it became a top five hit, and by Neil Diamond, again reaching the top of the charts, and by dozens of other artists. On the Hollies' version, Elton John played piano.

Scott was a jazz musician and songwriter from New York who toured with Louis Prima and Gene Krupa in the 1950s. He had a million seller in 1956 with "Chain Gang" and he won a Grammy Award for "Taste of Honey, performed by Herb Alpert. He died in 1990.

so prolific, or whatever the word is. A guy came to see us at the Whisky and he said he'd like us to come over to his studio and hear some songs, one in particular. "I'd like you guys to record it."

So here we were, big-time pot-smoking hippies from Minneapolis, we went over there. It was called El Dorado Studios, on Sunset and Vine. It was upstairs. Bobby Scott was his name. He played us a few of his songs, and then he said, "Now I want to play the song I'd like you to record. I think with your vocals, we could make this a hit." He gave us a cassette tape of it, and we took it home and listened to it. The big shots from Minnesota, "No, no, no, we can do our own songs, and we can do them better. We can do better than this."

The song was "He Ain't Heavy, He's My Brother."

Everything we got with Metromedia we fought for. That beautiful cover. Rico and Steve were down on Sunset Boulevard one day looking around. And there were these spinning carousels with postcards on them. Steve saw the Alphonse Mucha painting on one and said, "This is our album cover for Gypsy. It's perfect." So he buys four of the postcards and we take them up to the Valando brothers and tell them that this is what we want for the cover.

They looked into it, and it was $4,200 to get the rights to use it. And at that time it was a lot of money. Well, we got past that, and we had our cover. So now we're going to do the album and now we've got the cover.

We showed them songs. They had an A&R director whose name was Julio Aiello. He worked for Epic Records and then went to work for Metromedia because they thought they were going to sign more people. Julio became a very good friend of the band. He was a singer in his earlier years, a big band singer, and he loved the vocal thing.

Metromedia said we needed a photo for the centerfold of the cover. This photographer says, "Well, Gypsy, you guys should be out in the woods like you're traveling." So like Minnesota dumb asses, we drive into Forest Lawn cemetery. That's sacred ground out there. We get a bunch of pictures. The next thing, the cops drive up. They were going to arrest us because you're not supposed to be there. The photographer got us out of it. He told the cops what we were doing. The cops said, well this is private property, you can't be on it.

We went back and a few days later we saw the pictures, and we liked the one they used. Then we decided we wanted to have a matte finish, not a glossy finish like all the other album covers. Do you know how much that paper costs? It was like 21 cents per cover. But we talked and talked and talked, and we finally talked the Valando brothers into it.

Then we wanted the Gypsy on the cover to be embossed. They just looked at us and said, "Get the fuck out of the office." We figured we had gone as far as we could.

We went into the studio, Devonshire Sounds Studios on Magnolia Boulevard in North Hollywood, and everything's going good. It was a nice studio. We recorded every day there. Dave Mancini was the owner of the studio. He had this young kid that would come in every day and clean the studio. Everyday we'd get there and everything was cleaned up. This kid was doing this to earn studio time because he wanted to record some of his own songs. It was Billy Joel.

When we first went into the studio, of course, we did not know how to multi-track. We didn't know that trick. Nobody in Minnesota knew that trick. We all figured you recorded, and that was it. We get to Los Angeles, and the engineer says, "Well let's mult that." We didn't know what he was talking about. We wondered if we were going to have something to drink. He said, "No, we're going to mult it. Go in the studio again and sing it again. In stereo. Or three on this side and three on that side." Multi-tracking was big, and we learned that out there.

They gave us a credit card so that we could go to studio instrument rentals and get everything we needed. We got guitars, sound boards, whatever we needed.

Alphons Maria Mucha was a Czech painter and illustrator known for his theatrical posters done in Paris. His images became some of the best-known in the world in that time frame, the late 1800s and early 20th century. In addition to art, he trained as a pianist and violinist. In Munich, he received a commission to paint portraits of saints for a Czech church in Pisek, North Dakota, where they still are on display.
He moved to Paris in 1888 and his career soared after he created a series of posters for the actress Sarah Bernhardt.
The Gypsy illustration is officially known as "Zodiac" and features a beautiful woman surrounded by the signs of the Zodiac. This particular piece was done in 1896 or 1897. It was a poster and calendar done for La Plume Magazine, a literary and artistic review magazine published in Paris.
Gypsy still owns the rights to the Mucha illustration.

The interior artwork for the first Gypsy album was this photo taken at Forest Lawn Cemetery in Los Angeles. The police kicked them out, but not before this iconic image was made. From left: Jim Johnson, Jay Epstein, James Walsh, Doni Larson, Enrico Rosenbaum. (Metromedia)

We go down there and rented everything in the place. All the cool keyboards. We had 25 guitars at one time. Finally, they called us and yelled at us about that, "Look at this bill."

I think it took us three months in the studio. We had finished so many songs, but then we had to do the other part of the album. We'd fight with them all along the way. We'd play them things, like "Dead and Gone," and that's 11 minutes long. And they'd say, "What are you thinking? What about the radio?" We got past all that shit.

The album came out, and they didn't know what to do. They just didn't know what to do. Bobby Sherman had just been a built in. So we went back and got on their desk again. They did come through a little bit. There were some ads in Billboard newspaper. The album sold good enough for them to want to do a second one, but they told us in no uncertain terms that we are not going to do another double album. They gave us a $20,000 budget and so we went back into the studio.

We never had a hit. Our first album had started at 73. That was a big day in my life. I was at my parents' house and I got a call that said, "You're not going to believe this, but our fucking album just came onto Billboard." Usually you come on at a high number and work your way up. But we came on at 73. I said, are you kidding me? The reason we debuted so high was because Ira Heilicher, here in town, and his dad, Amos, owned Musicland record stores. Ira knew enough to take a big order. He bought like 7,500 copies. That was crazy. So all of a sudden, boom, we're on the chart. It made it up to 63.

"Dead and Gone" and "Gypsy Queen" were both released as singles. "Gypsy Queen" wasn't too bad because it had two parts, but "Dead and Gone" was stupid, it was eleven minutes. But the stations back then were different. We'd go out to KQRS in the Twin Cities at night with Alan Stone as the disc jockey, and we'd bring a brick of hash out there, and they'd play the whole fucking album. They just loved it. Same with St. Louis at KSHE. They just loved it. The DJs just loved it.

They had playlists back then, but they weren't created by some huge corporation. They were done at the station. A lot of DJs made hits. There was a guy up in Fargo, can't think of his name, made several big hits. He'd start playing a song, and it'd just suck down through Minnesota and the Midwest.

That's another part of this great big, nasty business. There are publishers in New York and L.A. that look for material for bands. If I call them up and say I'm Jimmy Walsh from Northeast Minneapolis and I'm looking for a song for my band, they would go down to drawer number four and say, oh, yeah, I've got these for you Jimmy Walsh from Northeast Minneapolis. If somebody from the Voice called, though, he would reach in the top drawer, his best songs. It's a making money thing.

Take iHeart, I don't know how many stations they own. And they're telling all of them what to play. Now, they not only control the stations, but they also control the concert venues. I don't know. I can't be down on it because I'm stuck with it.

In some ways, it's actually better these days because the artist can be more involved with their ca-

The first Gypsy album was recorded at Devonshire Studios in North Hollywood. The facility featured four sound recording studios. In addition to Gypsy, the studio produced albums by Billy Joel, Ringo Starr, the Jacksons, Bing Crosby, Green Day and Foo Fighters.
The studio since 1992 has been owned by Salami Studios and is used for cartoon voice-overs including SpongeBob SquarePants and Kung Fu Panda movies.

reers though the internet. Shania Twain and Prince were two of the first people who told their record companies, "Go fuck yourself. I'm not going to get ripped off anymore." Shania Twain put out an album by herself on the internet and sold as many copies as she would have normally, because she had a following. And so did Prince. He told Warner Brothers to go fuck themselves, and he changed his name to a symbol. It's better in some ways now. Back in the 70s, artists were just beginning to have more control.

It was not all a smooth ride. Jay Epstein had trouble in the studio playing Dead and Gone. It had a country beat. We got into a thing about this. It festered and festered and festered, and finally Jay said, "Fuck you, I'm leaving." Doni got caught up with that whole scene. He was a lesser influence on the music and consequently focused on the money and things. He decided to come home. So for the second album, we hired Bill Lordan on drums and Willie Weeks on bass, who were world class players. So in that respect, nothing lasts forever. Unless you're Jimmy Walsh.

We were recording one of the last two albums at RCA Record World on Sunset Boulevard. We had spent some time with the Tonight Show trumpet player Doc Severinsen, and he was recording the Last Tango in Paris soundtrack in Studio B and we were in Studio A. Studio B was a bigger room, size-wise because they had to get an orchestra in there. Our studio was technically the same, but it was smaller. We didn't need that much room. All of a sudden, he came through the door, and asked me if I wanted to play piano on this thing. I said, "Yeah, I'll play piano for a bit."

He came back and we got him really stoned. He snorted cocaine with us. He was all fucked up.

One day we were recording, and the studio guys came in and said, "We're going to stop for a little

Steven Stills

Richie Furay

Elvis Presley

Steven Stills wrote such classics as "For What It's Worth," "Love the One You're With," and "Suite: Judy Blue Eyes." He was part of Buffalo Springfield and Crosby, Stills, Nash and Young. Richie Furay was an important member of the early California rock and folk-rock scene and played in classic bands such as Buffalo Springfield and Poco. Elvis was, well, Elvis.

while." We wondered what the deal was and they said that Elvis was coming. This was before his comeback show in Los Vegas. He was still with RCA and they gave him Studio C to rehearse for that show. But while he came there, everything had to stop. They had a red carpet deal. He'd roll up in this big limousine, and everybody who was at the studio got to get in the receiving line. So I got to shake his hand. One day while they were there, I wandered over to Studio C and peeked in the door, and they were all in there watching porno movies. I went, "Oh, my God."

You knew every time he moved. Leaving was the same way. Nobody could go in or out. You stayed in your place. Security. He wasn't so fucked up then. Later on, we played the night before him at a place in Hawaii, but he was starting to fade by then, getting heavier.

One day, we were recording at RCA, and Richie Furay from Poco comes in. He said, "How you guys doing, what's going on? I need a keyboard player tonight, can you do it?" I said, "Hell, yes." So we hung around and there were other people who I can't remember, except that Stephen Stills came late. Richie was bitching at him for coming late because of studio time and stuff. We did this track, it was really nice. Now it's Stephen Stills turn. He'd been snorting cocaine all day long. He had this little bottle of coke, and he'd pour it out on his hand between his thumb and index finger and snort it up. He tried to do a snort, but he just couldn't do it. Finally, Richie Furay told him, "We'll try to do it another day, Steve, just try to get home safely." Stills started crying and he was all bummed out. I just left. I didn't want to see anymore.

Stills would have told you that at one point he was a complete fuck up and an ass. Something gets in your head, you turn into an ass.

COPPERHEAD
HNESSY HALL

is an eight-man group wit horn section a la Chicago and Ten Wheel Drive. The musicianship was at quite a high level but the group's original material was, for the most part, bland and uninspired. They did a lot of jamming but only seldom did anything worthwile come together.

Gypsy, a local group beginning to make it big nationally, was the evening's main attraction. Gypsy has been together eight or nine years, during most of which they were known as the Underbeats and were one of the top local groups. In fact, I remember them playing for a dance I attended in high school over six years ago. They were an animated jukebox then, doing cover versions of current hits and wearing matching suits.

They've come a long way since then. Almost all the material they now do is original and they have written some very nice songs. Their debut album, Gypsy, was released a few months ago and they have been playing prestigious

East in New York, where they reportedly were very well received.

The music is a successful blend of hard rock and softer, almost jazz-like strains. Their strongest point is the soaring harmony the vocalists have worked out. At times they sound almost as sweet as Crosby, Stills, Nash and Young. They all are good musicians but the lead guitarist was the outstanding and he doubled on flute and piano also.

JIM GILLESPIE is a Minneapolis free-lance reviewer of popular music.

Where Young plays beautiful cowboy music, Gypsy (formerly a local group, the Underbeats) plays polished tight rock bordering on jazz.

Their first album, GYPSY (Metromedia 1031), is a two-record set, an ambitious project for any group. Gypsy's music is tightly arranged, yet it flows very freely.

The song that is getting the most airplay is "Dead and Gone." It is long and suitelike, with an excellent piano solo and some lush three-part harmony.

That's just the word for Gypsy: lush. There is a soft touch to this group. It makes music that comes out and flows over you with a freshness and leisureliness that is very engaging.

Early Gypsy reviews from the *Minneapolis Star* and *Minneapolis Tribune* were very positive. On the left, Jim Gillespie said the group's "strongest point is the soaring harmony." On the right, Marshall Fine said, "That's just the word for Gypsy: lush."

Winterland, in San Francisco, where the manager for the Guess Who, Don Hunter, first saw Gypsy. He later bought out the rights to manage the band, and made them the opening act for the Guess Who. (Photo courtesy Jay Epstein)

CHAPTER SEVEN

ON THE ROAD WITH THE GUESS WHO

Anybody here see the noise, see the fear and commotion?
I think we missed it
Anybody here see the love, see the hate, the emotion?

Don't give me no hand me down shoes
Don't give me no hand me down love
Don't give me no hand me down world
I got one already
"Hand Me Down World"
— Kurt Winter, Guess Who, 1970

JAMES WALSH:

We got caught up with the Guess Who. The Guess Who thing sounded like a good idea, but it turned out to be not a good idea. Our momentum came to a great, slamming halt.

But it was an amazing experience. It all started when we played at Winterland in San Francisco. This venue was an offshoot by Bill Graham of his Fillmore West. He realized, and he was one of the early concert guys, that instead of having two thousand people, why don't I have 10,000 people? He was the innovator of all that shit.

This concert had the Guess Who, Gypsy, the Chambers Brothers and Mason Proffit. There were a lot of fucking people there. To make a long story short, the Guess Who's manager, Don Hunter, was there and he saw Gypsy. We were being booked out of L.A. by Jerry Heller and Don Fischel, and they were also booking the Guess Who. He saw us and really, really liked us.

The Guess Who, from left: Kurt Winter, Garry Peterson, Greg Leskiw, Burton Cummings, Jim Kale. Photo from July, 1970, just about the time Gypsy became their opening act. (Public domain)

The Guess Who originated in Winnipeg, Canada, and at one point were known as Chad Allan and the Reflections. They had a cover hit, "Shakin' All Over" in 1965 but the record company wanted to convince the American record buyers that this was a British invasion group and so the band's name was listed as "Guess Who?" After a disastrous tour of England, the band hired Don Hunter as manager, and did TV house band work for several years. In 1969, they released *Wheatfield Soul* and the single "These Eyes," and the Guess Who, who had dropped the question mark a couple of years earlier, hit the big time. Burton Cummings, the lead singer, and guitarist Randy Bachman were the creative dynamos in the group, but Bachman left in 1970 to form Bachman-Turner Overdrive. The band continued to turn out hits like, "American Woman," "Share the Land," and "Laughin'" but never was able to crack album rock radio. In the early 70s, the band became more progressive, much like the band they toured with, Gypsy, but were still unable to escape their reputation as a pop band. Perhaps one reason Cummings and James Walsh became friends was because they were both several years younger than other members of their bands, and they were both keyboardists who had quit high school to do music full time. By 1975, when Cummings quit and the band broke up, they were called by McLean's, a Canadian magazine, "fat, sloppy and undisciplined." They also had a reputation for imbibing large quantities of soft drugs and alcohol, the magazine said.

In their heyday, they had 14 charted hits in the United States and 30 in Canada, and they were the first Canadian group to have a number-one album in the United States. Canadian fans feel it is a snub that the group has never been inducted into the Rock and Roll Hall of Fame.

About a month later, we got a call from him, and he told us that the Guess Who had bought the management of our band. At the time, we thought it was great. After time, we realized it was one of those mistakes we made. We were stupid and didn't have good management. They bought out our manager for $15,000, which was a lot of money then. They took over management of the band. They were in Winnipeg and we were in Minneapolis. They liked Winnipeg because it was in the center of the continent, and you could travel from there to anywhere.

We traveled with them to every major city, every secondary city, every college, and every secondary college. We went everywhere. We thought, "Oh, my God, we're going to be seen by thousands and thousands of people. We each got $175 a week, the whole band. I was living up in Polynesian Village in St. Anthony Village, and that paid for my apartment and then some.

They just called Concerts West and said that from now on our opening act will be Gypsy, and we thought, "Oh, wow, this is going to be great, all that exposure." As it turned out, though, we should have stayed on our own and looked for a new deal with someone who would promote us. We should have taken that Atlantic deal, we should have done a lot of things. We were just stupid.

What we were really good at was stealing the Guess Who's identity. We traveled with them everywhere. We found out that all you had to do was, when you went into a restaurant, to just say "We're with the Guess Who" and they would be billed. We all looked the same. The waiter wouldn't know. We ran up a $600 bill in Denver one time. We had a $450 bill somewhere else.

One of their guitar players, Kurt Winter, just bugged us. We got to a hotel one night, a Holiday Inn-type place, and we got all four of our rooms to boil water in the coffee makers. So we had a significant amount of boiling water in a little waste can. We went down to his door, leaned the water can against the door, pounded on it, and when he opened the door, all this boiling water went on his bare feet. Oh, we got in so

Don Hunter became Gypsy's manager in 1970 and immediately made the band the opening act for the other group he managed, the Guess Who. Hunter was a former lounge singer, vending machine salesman and bowling champion in Winnipeg who formed the Quasimodo Agency in 1967, the same year he signed the Guess Who. A Winnipeg rocker named John Einerson, who was also managed by Hunter, said he was "a larger than life character, abrasive at times and physically intimidating." But he also, "was a lovable guy with a good heart." Hunter loved to sing and write poetry, and he enjoyed the life of a rock band manager including dinner at the White House when the Guess Who played for Princess Anne and the Prince of Wales. He died in 2019, and his obituary said that in his later years, living on a farm, he would entertain friends by breaking out cassette tapes of his favorite bands, including Gypsy.

The Guess Who toured the United States and Canada almost continuously during their heyday. One stop was at the St. Paul Auditorium. Their opening act was nearly always Gypsy.

much trouble for that. We got a water damage bill. He wouldn't talk to us for a long time except to say, "You guys are fucked." But basically, they were Canadians, they were good guys. They weren't jerks.

We didn't get into too much trouble on the road. We were Minnesota Nice. We were just a bunch of farmers from Minnesota trying to take in this strange dream on the West Coast. We were good boys.

Lynyrd Skynyrd and those types of bands were crazy, just crazy. We never did anything like that. The Guess Who were the same as us. However, they were absolute Canadian drunks. Kurt Winter, the guy whose feet we boiled, didn't use his bathtub in the hotels. That was one of the things that bugged us about him. He wore the same Garnet Amp t-shirt for two years. You'd go in his room, and his tub was full of ice and beer. Jim Kale was the same way. Ice and beer, and they just drank. We weren't like that. We weren't drinkers. We had it in our rider, though, that Gypsy would receive beer, pop, Captain Morgan and other stuff. It's just asking for trouble. They treated bands pretty well in those days. I can show you our rider from that time. There was a significant amount of liquor involved.

We smoked a lot of hash with the Guess Who. Burton Cummings, the lead singer, had a lot of money, and he would buy Nepalese finger hash. It was the best stuff you could get. It would come in a statue and the fingers were full of hash. You would take a hammer and break it off, and there would be a finger of hash. We'd go to his room late at night, and he'd take a screw, and screw it in the end. We'd light the other side, and it would burn for hours. We'd sit in his room, and sometimes put it under a glass and then inhale it.

In Canada, there's not a lot of high quality roads to move around with our music equipment. And so they leased us a Boeing 737 for the two bands. We could go from one town to another, and there was no problem. You could leave anytime you wanted.

We were in Burton Cummings room one night, all in a circle, smoking a finger. I'm passing the finger to the guy next to me, and I look and it's the pilot of the plane. The next guy was the co-pilot of the plane.

The next morning we get up and head for the plane. There were no gateways, we'd just have to walk out on the tarmac and climb the stairs to the plane. The last two guys on the plane are the two pilots. I'm thinking, "What am I doing here?" They wouldn't drink, but they would smoke. They must have been having a fucking ball up there flying that jet around. We did that several times.

I'd hear the engine revving up, and I'd say, "Here we go, God."

We played once in Sun Valley, Idaho, at Sun Valley Resort. Somebody had rented this piece of land. We flew in there on a six-passenger twin engine plane. I hate small planes. We flew over the site. We came into this valley between two large mountain ranges. It was a huge venue. We figured this was another Woodstock or Atlanta Pop Festival. We could see bathrooms lined up for miles. There were no people, just bathrooms.

We landed and went to the gig, and nobody came. Maybe 200 people. They had enough bathrooms for about 300,000 people. They built it and nobody came.

I don't remember the bands that were playing there, but Wolfman Jack was the emcee. He was a big deal back then. He had at least two or three trailers, motorhomes, with him just for his entourage.

They had a complaint because these motorhomes were sucking all the juice out of these portable generators. When we got on stage, I started my organ and it was just making a sound like, eeeeaaaeeeya, eeeeyaeeya, eeyaeeeeeeeyaeeyaeeya. We finally realized that there's just not enough power. So I went and talked with Wolfman to see if we could unplug a couple of the trailers and he said okay. Then the organ would work.

Robert Weston Smith was born in Brooklyn, New York, in 1938 and in the early 60s took on the moniker "Wolfman Jack" and became a full-time disc jockey. He became famous as a DJ at XERF-AM broadcasting from Mexico, just across the border from Texas. The station, illegal by American standards, had 250,000 watts, five times what was allowed in the United States, and could be heard from coast to coast. His style was unique, aggressive, and often laced with sexual undertones. In the mid-60s, he was hired to manage KUXL in Minneapolis, which at that time had an R&B format. Wolfman reached the pinnacle of his fame playing himself in the movie "American Graffiti" in 1973. The Guess Who in 1974, while still touring with Gypsy, wrote one of their later, minor hits, "Clap for the Wolfman."

There were these people out in front of the stage, and it was such a small crowd that you could count them, but Wolfman went on like nothing was wrong. The people sat right down in front and they had a firepit going and they were cooking food. They brought him up some fish they were cooking, and I remember him saying, "Save some fish for the band." We never saw any fish.

The Guess Who and Gypsy were trail blazers in Las Vegas. The Las Vegas Convention Center at one time booked Sly Stone, but he didn't show up. He put up a retainer of $10,000 saying that he'd come back and make it up to the fans. He didn't show up again. The fans tore this fucking place apart. The powers that be in Las Vegas said, "Fuck this concert shit. These musicians are crazy." Don Heller and Jerry Fischel went to Las Vegas and talked to the commission, or whoever it was, and they told them that they could bring in a clean show. They said, "We want to re-establish concerts in your city." Some time had gone by, a couple or three years, since they allowed any concerts.

The guys in Las Vegas took them at their word and booked the Guess Who and Gypsy. The guys in the band didn't know, but this was a big deal in Las Vegas. When the plane landed, the stewardess said, "Will the members of Guess Who and Gypsy please stay on board." We thought, "Well, okay."

We got off the plane and the whole airport is lined with people. All the way down the concourse were people. From the time we got off the plane until we reached Caesar's Palace, it was all people. The news media were all there. We had three limos for the bands, and when we got to Caesar's Palace, there was another throng of people waiting for us. We're going, "What the fuck is going on here?" They took us into Caesar's Palace into a room and sat us all down for a news conference. And the questions were about how we were going to act, and we told them how we weren't going to fuck this up. That was quite an experience. We just didn't know about this big stink, and that we were the first band coming back after this trouble.

So the Guess Who was staying at Caesar's Palace,

and Gypsy was staying at Eddie's Used Saddle Shop and Motel. Burton Cummings says to me, "Well why don't you just stay in my room? I said okay. Then he says, "Why don't we go downstairs and gamble?" I said I'd like to, but I didn't have any money. He said okay and he gave me a thousand dollars. I'm in good shape. I made back the thousand and made 600 bucks. But he's ruining it for me, because he's drunk. He's got 16 up and the dealer has a five and Burton is saying, "Give me a hit, give me a hit." I said to Burton, "You've got to wait it out, just wait it out." But he was drunk and he didn't care. He lost thousands of dollars. That was a good time for him.

We went to Hawaii with them twice. I was with Burton Cummings and some guy I can't remember, and Cummings was getting drunk. We got in the cab, and he transformed himself into Richard Burton, the actor. He had that aristocratic accent, and he was really into it. Finally the cab driver just pulled over and said, "Get out." I said, "I told you." He just got drunk, he got drunk all the time.

He owned a house up in Winnipeg, a big beautiful house, and you'd walk in the door and it's white. There's nothing in the house. No pictures, no furniture, not a stitch. Until you got to his bedroom, and that was all decked out, grand piano, big TV. But there was nothing in the rest of the house.

Don Hunter went to RCA, who were the label for the Guess Who, and we signed a contract. We did *Antithesis* and *Unlock the Gates*. That was good, but we never spun out of that with any momentum.

All that time in California. I know there were good times, but sometimes I look back and say I hated every minute of it. The band had run its course, four albums, made a bunch of bad decisions. Nothing happened. Then we broke up. Minds had diverted in different ways. Rico was involved with this girl, and he got involved with heroin.

I decided to come home. I decided I was done with this shit, and I'm going home.

Jerry Heller and Don Fischel formed their agency in 1970 and began booking many of the major acts of the time, including The Guess Who, The Who, Humble Pie, Van Morrison,Cat Stevens, Grassroots, Lee Michaels and Gypsy. Heller, a native of Cleveland, previously worked for Associated Booking and Chartwell but told Billboard in1970 that he split off because he felt bands needed agents that knew their music and related to them. Fischel, formerly of William Morris Agency, was known for his booking expertise. Heller later went on as one of the first bookers of rap acts in the 1980s, providing momentum for such acts as Dr. Dre, Ice Cube, and N.W.A. In later years, the artists accused Heller of taking advantage of them. He is featured in the movie "Straight Outta Compton" portrayed by Paul Giamatti.

Returning from Los Angeles and the breakup of Gypsy, Walsh next worked with the band Free and Easy, managed by Thomas Behr. Behr and Walsh disagreed on the direction of the band, and Behr took the name of the band and departed. The Walsh group became the James Walsh Gypsy Band. (Photo courtesy minniepaulmusic.com)

CHAPTER EIGHT

TROUBLE WITH THE LAW

Busted, down on Bourbon Street
Set up, like a bowlin' pin
Knocked down, it gets to wearin' thin
They just won't let you be

Truckin', I'm a goin' home
Whoa, whoa, baby, back where I belong
Back home, sit down and patch my bones
And get back truckin' on

— Jerry Garcia, Philip Lesh, Robert Hunter, Bob Weir
Grateful Dead, 1970

JAMES WALSH:

I might have been an asshole.

I fell into the Hollywood deal. I thought my shit didn't stink. I was receiving $1,200 a week in royalty checks. I was a young guy. I was playing and making money and living in Hollywood. I lived next door to Micky Dolenz and Frank Zappa.

And then we go out on tour with the Guess Who for two and one half years. I had grown up a little bit, and the age separation between the older guys and myself had leveled off. I took a more important position in the band. When Jim came back, Rico and I had kind of taken over, and Jim and Rico both realized my ability to arrange music and write music.

When the bottom fell out for Gypsy in 1974, I decided to come home. I really didn't have a plan. I brought my family home, and we had a place on 23rd and Arthur in Northeast Minneapolis, right on the corner – a stucco duplex upstairs.

I got a job playing with the Accents, one of the premiere bands of the 60s in the Twin Cities. This version had Tom Nystrom, Ken Sand, Bobby Jones and me, but the band was just about done.

I was faced with trying to maintain a lifestyle. You know, Gypsy had enjoyed a modicum of success. When I got home, that came to an abrupt, deadly halt. So I said, well, I'll just sell some baggies to my friends. So I sold some pot, and then I sold some cocaine. I was doing really good until November of 1975. And then the whole world changed again. That house of cards came down quickly.

I opened the back door one day and the guy put a gun on my forehead, not near it, on it. He said, "Back up, fatso, or I'm going to blow your fucking head off." So I backed up to the refrigerator. He identified himself as a federal agent. I told him, "There are children in the home and there are no guns here. I would appreciate it if you would lower your weapon." So he did.

So they came into my house. They found three pounds of pot, forty-eight grams of cocaine, two scales, two pounds of mannitol, which is the cutting material for cocaine. That was kind of a turning point for me. I remember sitting at the kitchen table. I had just sent Rico and Sam out the front door with two pounds of pot. Luckily they didn't see that or they would have grabbed them too.

The United States Federal Office Building in downtown Minneapolis, later known as the Old Federal Building.

There were other band members in the living room. I said, "Let them go, they have nothing to do with my shit. Just let them go." So they let them go. So I'm sitting at the kitchen table. The guy's got a gun on me. He looked around and saw it was he and I alone. He said, "I want to tell you something, Walsh." I figured I was going to get some kind of routine. He said, "You guys opened for Steppenwolf at the Convention Center. You were awesome. You guys were great." So he's got a gun on me. I told him, "Well I appreciate that, but a lot of good it's going to do me now."

They arrested me. They were nice enough to not handcuff me when we left the house. I asked if they had a search warrant and they didn't. I went downtown. I spent from about 4:30 in the afternoon to about nine or ten that night, and they were interrogating me. They were asking me to give somebody up. They said, "The more you tell us, the less trouble you're in." I decided at that point not to go that route. I knew there would always be that opportunity later. I asked for an attorney, so they took me over to the courthouse. I went upstairs, all the way up to the jail there. They put me in a cell.

I'm a wreck, because I've never been in trouble. I'm just a wreck. I look up and I see there's a TV and Channel 4 is on. I thought, "Well, at least I can sit here and watch TV." All of a sudden it's 10 o'clock, lights go dark and the TV goes off.

Now I'm sitting there. I had hair down to my waist. The curly locks had turned into four nervous strands of hair. I sat on the edge of the bunk, I never laid down. At six in the morning, a guy whisks by my cell and throws a roll into me in a cellophane wrapper. It hits the floor. The roll comes out of the wrapper and slams into the toilet. He said, "Good morning, breakfast."

I was sick. I was in so much fucking trouble.

I had been a good kid, an athlete. I had never done anything bad. At 11 a.m., the cell door opens and they told me my family had bailed me out. I had made my one call to my brother. They took me out of the cell and put handcuffs on me and they said that we're going over to the Federal Building. I thought, well, that's okay, we're going to get in the car and go to the federal building. Instead, they walked me to the Federal Building through downtown Minneapolis. It was going on noon, and the big city streets were bustling. Four guys and me, the guy in the handcuffs, in the middle. We came up to the stop sign, and people were just separating. It was the worst day of my life.

They let me go, and I found out my family had hired Doug Thompson as my attorney. He was the number one guy. He was the top defense attorney in Minnesota. They told me I had to go to his office right away, so I drove over to St. Paul. I sat with him. He said, "I'm not really interested in what you have to say. You're a dumb ass, and you're in a lot of trouble, and I'm going to try and get you out of trouble. But don't give me any of your sad stories." I said, "Okay."

He said, "You live in a duplex. All you had to do was keep that stuff in the attic, and you'd be walking right now." He lectured me for a little while and talked about different things, and I said, "I got to know how much this is going to cost me." He said, "Seventy-five hundred bucks." Well, this was 1975, that's like $75,000 now. I said, "Okay."

I knew I had some money at home, so I asked him how long I had to get this money together. He

Judge Miles Lord graduated from the University of Minnesota Law School in 1948. He was in private practice and served as a United States Attorney before being elected Minnesota's Attorney General in 1955. He served for five years. He was appointed a United States District Court judge in 1966 by President Lyndon Johnson. He served as Chief Judge of that court from 1981-1985. He was regarded as a tough judge and was greatly involved in the Reserve Mining Company decision in 1973, requiring the mining company to quit dumping taconite waste into Lake Superior. He also tried the Dalkon Shield case, finding against the intrauterine device manufacturers to the tune of $220 million. He did a private practice after his retirement and died in 2016.

looked at his watch and said, "How about 45 minutes?" I said, "I gotta go." I came back a couple of hours later and I had the money.

Thompson said, "What I want you to do is to right away get into a band. Right away. Don't get a speeding ticket. I'm going to keep this out of court, I'm going to let this all fester down. Then we'll go back into court and we'll plead guilty and take what we get."

A friend of mine, Jimi Behringer, asked me to join the band Free and Easy. I was lying low, so this was perfect. I could make some money. It was a great band, great musicians, good people.

My arraignment came in Minneapolis. I was sitting in the courtroom with Thompson. I look up on the bench, and who's there but Miles Lord, the hanging judge. He had just given the guy before me seven years. Thompson and I are looking at each other, and he's shaking his head and I know exactly why.

The guy who got seven years, his attorney asked Judge Lord if he could give himself up after Christmas so he could spend that time with his family before he went to prison. Lord looked down and then slammed his gavel and said, "Merry Christmas, Bobby. Take him away."

My knees are knocking together. Now, it's my turn and I get arraigned and I plead not guilty, and Judge Lord said, "You know, I'd like to have you in jail before Christmas too." My heart just sank. I was in a lot of trouble. Thompson and I went out in the hallway, and he said, "Well this isn't a good sign." I said, "Well you didn't have to tell me that."

Miraculously, Doug Thompson somehow moved my case to St. Paul. To this day, I don't know how. I've talked to other lawyers, and they don't know how he did it either. But he did it. He got me away from Judge Lord. The new guy was Judge Donald Alsop who had just left his private practice in New Ulm. He later succeeded Lord as the chief judge of the Minnesota district court. Thompson said, "This is a good guy. He thinks a little differently. He's more compassionate."

We went upstairs to the pre-sentence investigator, and this guy's got on a polka dot shirt and plaid pants. He looked like a drill sergeant. The first thing he said was, "Why don't you cut that fucking hair?" He started filling out my paperwork, and he suddenly looked up. "What are you doing here? You're not supposed to be here. You're supposed to be in Minneapolis. I can't deal with this. Go to Minneapolis."

I went to Minneapolis the next day which turned out to be a life-saving event. I'm sitting outside the probation office, waiting, and around the corner came this beautiful, young woman. I was looking at her, of course. I looked at every girl. She's walking, walking, walking, and all of a sudden she's in front of me. She said, "Are you James Walsh?" and I said, "Yes I am." She said, "Let's go in my office, I'm going to handle your pre-sentence investigation."

I swear to you, the first thing she said to me was, "Are you Gypsy?" I said, "Yeah." And she said, "I love your music. I just love your music." So the devil in me is thinking different things. We had her over to my house and she met my parents. One day she said, "Would you like to come over to my house? I have a place down on the St. Croix."

I thought about it. And I thought, "Don't go. Just don't go." I said, "I don't think that's appropriate at this particular time." That turned out to be a test she was giving me, a moral character test to see if I was a sleazeball, or if I had some kind of redeeming quality. She did up my pre-sentence investigation three days before my hearing.

Since we now had Alsop as the judge, we decided to waive my right to a trial and just let the judge handle the decision. So three days before the hearing, Thompson and I sat in Alsop's office. The judge said, "You've done well in the pre-sentence phase. You've done very well.

"You're going to get three years.

"You'll go to prison for three years, but if you're

Donald Alsop grew up in Duluth and graduated from the University of Minnesota Law School in 1952. He served in the Army at the end of World War II. He was in private practice in New Ulm in 1975, when he was chosen by President Richard Nixon to serve on the United States District Court for the District of Minnesota. Nixon made the choice on the day before he resigned from office. There were 21 lawyers from Minnesota vying for the post, but Nixon chose Alsop. He was confirmed with the help of Minnesota Senators Hubert Humphrey and Walter Mondale, despite the fact that Alsop was a Republican. Alsop later replaced Miles Lord as the chief judge for Minnesota. Among the important cases in his tenure was the Virginia Piper kidnapping trial. He also was involved in the Dalkon Shield case that Lord presided over. He retired as chief judge in 1992 and became a senior judge at that point. He enjoyed presiding over naturalization ceremonies, welcoming new citizens to good, you'll get out a little sooner."

Now I'm at the bottom of the barrel again. I'm not floating right above the bottom, I'm on the bottom. For three days. I was thinking, "My next sexual encounter is going to be with a guy named Chuck. I'm going to be somebody's bitch, I'm going to be making somebody's bunk." For three days, I don't sleep. My parents want to know what's going on, but I didn't tell them anything.

I went down to the courthouse myself. I remember taking my dad's car to St. Paul, parking it in a lot near the courthouse. I told my dad where it was and I left the keys under the mat. I went upstairs.

Alsop said, "Do you have anything to say?" I gave him about a 20-minute dissertation on what an idiot I was. This whole process had taken about three years to get to this point. I just told the judge it was a big mistake on my part.

Alsop said, "Well, Mr. Walsh, you don't have any priors, and I've studied the case. I'm sentencing you to three years – stayed sentence." I didn't know what that meant. So I'm already getting my hands behind my back so they can put on the handcuffs. Thompson said, "Let's go." I said, "I don't know what's going on." Thompson said, "He stayed your sentence for three years." He gave me a year's probation. With all that shit.

We got out in the hallway. Thompson said, "Before the hearing, I went into the judge's chamber and read the letter the pre-sentence investigator had written. It was like a love letter from heaven. It said that under no uncertain terms should you jail this person. He's not a threat to society. He's made mistakes. He's a good person. I love his music."

Now I'm driving down 94, heading home, and I'm going about 90. I didn't care if I got a speeding ticket.

The next week, I went to see this woman who had written my pre-sentence investigation. I thanked her. I told her that I understood the letter was very upbeat. "Yeah," she said. "I thought you were worth saving." She looked at me, this beautiful woman, and said she wanted me to fill out a form. So I did. I signed my name at the bottom. She said, "You don't have to come back. I'll fill out your probation form every month." I never saw her again. I never went back.

Talk about praying.

Walsh left Free and Easy and the new group was the James Walsh Gypsy Band. Their single, "Cuz It's You Girl" had some regional success. (Photo courtesy James Walsh)

Chapter Nine

Muscle Shoals

Now Muscle Shoals has got the Swampers
And they've been known to pick a song or two (yes they do)
Lord they get me off so much
They pick me up when I'm feelin' blue
Now how about you?
— Sweet Home Alabama, Lynyrd Skynyrd, 1974
Edward King, Gary Rossington, Ronnie Van Zant

James Walsh:

When I was laying low with my legal troubles, Jimi Behringer asked me to join Free and Easy. I could make some money. It was perfect for me. And then I wrote, "Cuz It's You Girl."

I had a good friend from Columbia Heights, Ron Geslin, who at the time was the vice president of promotion for RCA. He had been in the Hot Half Dozen with me some years before. After my little thing with the law, 1975 to 1977, I stayed in contact with him. And I sent him a demo of "Cuz It's You Girl."

He took it to Warren Schatz, who was the head of A&R at RCA, and Warren said it was a hit song. He just fell in love with the song. He came to Minneapolis and I signed a contract with him at the White Castle on Central Avenue in Northeast. We had reservations for Charlie's Café downtown, which at that time was the place to go in the Twin Cities, and he said, "No, no, no, I've got all the paperwork here, let's go to White Castle." So I sat at White Castle on Central Avenue and signed a two-record deal with RCA Records.

The band was Free and Easy, but Schatz wanted to call it Gypsy, because there was some name

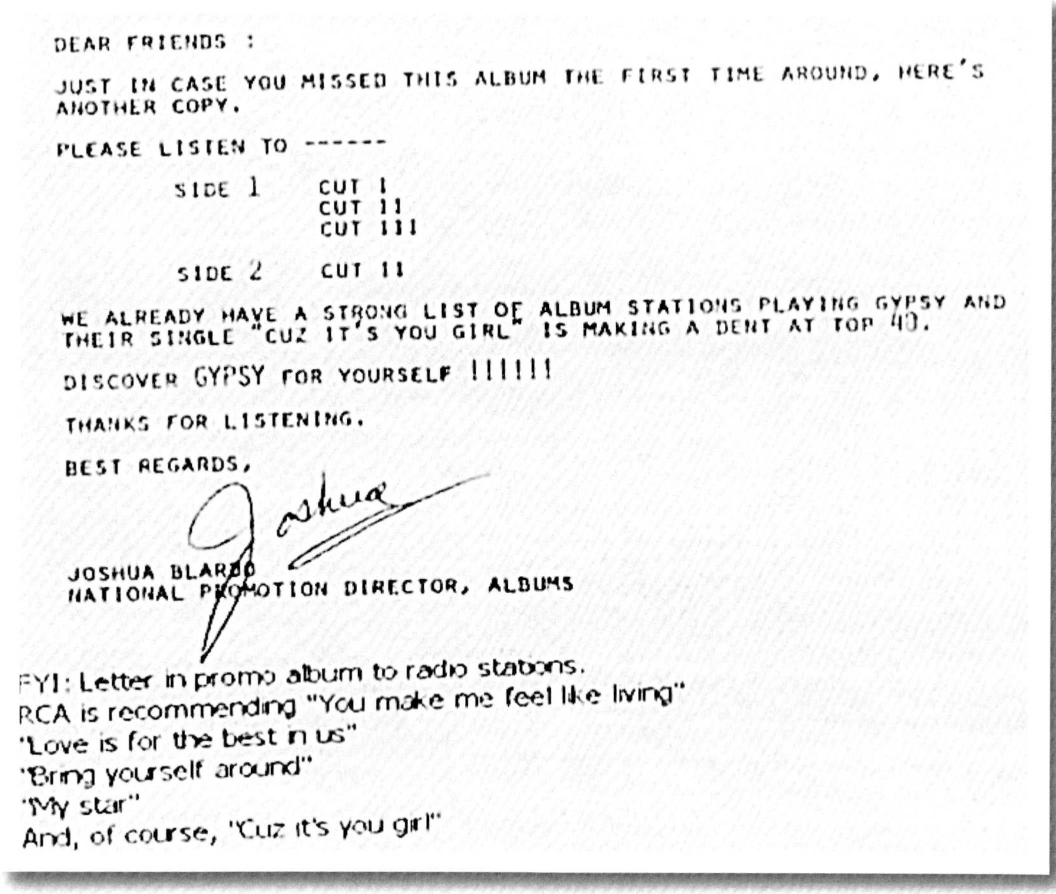

DEAR FRIENDS :

JUST IN CASE YOU MISSED THIS ALBUM THE FIRST TIME AROUND, HERE'S ANOTHER COPY.

PLEASE LISTEN TO ------

SIDE 1 CUT I
CUT II
CUT III

SIDE 2 CUT II

WE ALREADY HAVE A STRONG LIST OF ALBUM STATIONS PLAYING GYPSY AND THEIR SINGLE "CUZ IT'S YOU GIRL" IS MAKING A DENT AT TOP 40.

DISCOVER GYPSY FOR YOURSELF !!!!!!

THANKS FOR LISTENING.

BEST REGARDS,

Joshua

JOSHUA BLARDO
NATIONAL PROMOTION DIRECTOR, ALBUMS

FYI: Letter in promo album to radio stations.
RCA is recommending "You make me feel like living"
"Love is for the best in us"
"Bring yourself around"
"My star"
And, of course, "Cuz it's you girl"

After the first James Walsh Gypsy Album was released, the marketing department at RCA Records swung into action. "Cuz It's You Girl" was on the charts, but RCA's Joshua Blardo, a national promotion director for albums, sent out this note to radio stations across the country. The letter asks the radio guys to try out other songs on the album. (Courtesy James Walsh)

The James Walsh Gypsy Band toured extensively promoting their new album. This stop was at the Union Bar in downtown Minneapolis. The Daisy Dillman Band, a rock and country band with lush vocals, also made an RCA album at Muscle Shoals, but with Rick Hall at Fame Studios. The band played for 46 years and announced its retirement in 2022.

recognition. And so we called it the James Walsh Gypsy Band. Another coup. We played a lot of other material, but we played mostly Gypsy songs. We did some horn songs.
I told the guys in the band, I don't know what you guys want to do, but I know what I'm going to do. I'm going to sign a record contract. I'll give you a couple of hours to make up your mind if you want to do this. Everybody called except two guys, and we went on from there. Bobby Jones from Northeast came with the band then, and he's been with me for a number of years. We got a new drummer, Ernie LaViolette, who was great. We toured all over with that band.

In 1978, we released the album featuring "Cuz It's You, Girl." The single was on the Billboard charts for seven weeks and made it up to number 71. It did pretty well, but at that time RCA decided to dump 30 artists. That was the time of the fuel crisis and inflation and all that crap. I thought for sure that they would let me go, because there were bigger names, but they stuck with me. We had a two-record deal.

So they called and asked, do I have more songs? I said, of course I do. They said, "Here's what we're going to do. We're going to send you to Muscle Shoals. We want to get you with some world-class producers." Jimmy Johnson and Barry Beckett were about as world class as you could get. I almost fell out of my chair. I got a call from Jimmy Johnson, and he said they agreed to take on the album. I was very surprised. I said, "Well, what's the budget going to be?" and he said, "Oh, we've got $135,000." But they said, we don't want you to use your band. We want you to use the Muscle Shoals Rhythm Section — the Swampers.

So I had to make a very painful decision right then. I talked to several people about it. I talked to my dad about it. And I talked to Ron Geslin about it. It was just an opportunity I couldn't pass up. So I took Jim Behringer and Bobby Jones with me. Bobby to sing and Jim to play guitar. That way there would be some continuity with the old stuff and the new stuff.

The project included the Muscle Shoals guys, the two

Warren Schatz was born in Brooklyn, New York, in 1945, and started his musical career as a delivery boy for Associated Recording. He soon found a slot as an engineer at the studio, and recorded demos for such artists as Paul Simon, Neil Diamond, Dionne Warwick and Carole King. He also recorded his own music on several labels. He had a career in Europe and lived in Helsinki, Finland, for a time. Returning to the U.S., he did arrangements for Tony Orlando and Frankie Valli. He became national vice president of A&R at RCA in 1976 and worked with Hall and Oates and others. It was during this stint that he signed James Walsh to a two-record deal with RCA. He was prominent in the rise and fall of disco music in the 1970s.

Jimi Behringer grew up in Minneapolis and started playing guitar at age 10. He played in his brother's band and in other local bands, before working with his dad in manufacturing bicycles. During the 70s he came back to music, his first love, and joined the band Good Vibrations and later Free and Easy.

In addition to the James Walsh Gypsy Band, he played and wrote songs with many local and national artists including Prince, where he played session guitar on "The Most Beautiful Girl in the World." He toured with Laura Branigan, and appeared on the Tonight Show. Other artists he played with and wrote songs with included Willie Murphy, the Steeles and Ricky Peterson. He created two of his own albums.

Gypsy guys, and they added on all the other stuff. At the beginning, our road manager Chopper Black was also there and our manager Cliff Siegal was there. We moved into a house down there and it was very nice. We moved into the lower level, and Bob Seger was on the upper level. There was a cook for everybody every day, which was really nice. There was maid service.

We spent a few weeks down there, and then the Gypsy band went back out on tour promoting the previous CD. All the gigs were out east somewhere. What happened, those guys went from the tour back home, and I went back to Muscle Shoals by myself. So Bob Seger and I lived together for three months. He was a fabulous guy. His manager, Punch Andrews, was with him. We did everything together every day.

Muscle Shoals Sound Studio had purchased a National Guard Armory on the Tennessee River. They put a four-walled studio in the middle of this huge building. So when you walked in you could see the four walls of this studio. They had basketball courts. They had punching bags. They had two back-to-back studios, identical. They had all the best equipment. They had two 24-track recorders in each room. Because of the remote location, they had also built in a complete studio instrument rentals facility. They had every instrument you can imagine. Maybe five drum sets. They had three organs, they had several different style pianos, they had 25 acoustic guitars, they had 25 electric guitars, 25 amplifier choices. So people didn't have to bring their own stuff in. It was a great facility, they had a kitchen, they had couches. Those guys were all very good, they were all down home, really good musicians. You could go on and on forever about what they had done. They had one gold record every month for 10 years.

Once we decided we were going to do it, Barry Beckett and Jimmy Johnson wanted to have input on the song selection. Of course, I said, "Fine." So they presented some songs. I can't remember the balance, but I ended up with half and they ended up with half.

While I was there, Warner Brothers came in and gave

the Swampers this anniversary dinner, and awarded them all these gold records. My timing was right and I got to go to the dinner. They had worked with everybody. The engineers were great, the studio was great, the best I got from it was that I sat and listened. I sat and learned. I saw how they were making records. I learned a lot from that. It was a great experience.

Everything about Muscle Shoals was fantastic. The food was fantastic. The town was fantastic. It was a no alcohol town, so they'd have to drive to Tennessee to get liquor. There were no drugs down there, but the engineer was a cocaine head, and they all smoked pot. To be honest, I think that was part of the creativity down there. They were coming to work every day getting high, playing with the Rolling Stones, Bob Seger and all these other people, and it was a ball.

It was just a better experience in the studio. When we did the first four albums, it was more of a hit and miss thing when we went in the studio every day. We were experimenting in the studio. It was a bad, bad, bad idea. Nobody knew any better. We had picked the songs, but picking songs is different than recording songs. When I got to Muscle Shoals, it was like clockwork. They didn't waste any time on anything. You started, you stopped, went and ate, started again, stopped, every aspect of that was planned out. That's how we do it now. I give the guys the songs, or in some cases, they come in and I have all the parts. It's very simple. I break it down to three or four parts. We learn those parts very quickly, and here's the progression of those parts. So it goes quick. It's easy if you've got good musicians, and they listen. The Muscle Shoals guys were so used to each other, they moved slowly, but it was clockwork for them.

They were really nice guys. Down home guys, like Northeasters. They weren't pompous asses. You'd walk into the studio, in the lobby and the walls were full, right next to each other, gold record, gold record, gold record. You just went whoa.

You just learn, you know, multi-track recording. At the time there were machines that could do reverb, but the Muscle Shoals guys didn't like those ma-

Bob Seger was born in 1945 in Detroit and achieved local fame in the 1960s. In the 70s he put together the Silver Bullet Band, all Detroit musicians, and his 1975 album *Night Moves* put him on the national map. He also worked extensively with the Muscle Shoals Rhythm Section, often called the Swampers.
In 1979, when he shared a house with James Walsh in Sheffield, Alabama, he was recording the album *Against the Wind* at Muscle Shoals. The album didn't win unanimous critical acclaim, but it did win two Grammy awards that year. It sold over five million copies and was Seger's only number one Billboard album listing. Seger was elected to the Rock and Roll Hall of Fame in 2004 and the Song Writers Hall of Fame in 2012. He announced his retirement in 2018.

In 1979, the Muscle Shoals Rhythm Section, the Swampers, outgrew their iconic building in Sheffield, Alabama, and purchased a former National Guard building nearby and installed two studios in its spacious interior. The James Walsh album, which was never released at the time, was recorded there. The Swampers were four musicians from the area, Barry Beckett, Roger Hawkins, Jimmy Johnson and David Hood. They were the main rhythm section for Rick Hall's FAME Studios and produced many hits before breaking out on their own. They were the first group of musicians to own a studio. Jerry Wexler of Atlantic Records partnered with the Swampers in their new venture and sent many recording artists their way. Their first album was for Cher in 1969. In the coming years, they recorded Wilson Pickett, Aretha Franklin, the Staple Singers, the Rolling Stones, Duane Allman, Elton John, Boz Scaggs, Willie Nelson, Paul Simon and many others. Their first hit on their own was R.B. Greaves' "Take a Letter, Maria." They recorded Bob Dylan's "Slow Train Coming" and the Stones' "Wild Horses" and "Brown Sugar." Over the years, they were involved with 75 recordings that went gold or platinum.

chines. So what they did was they built a series of home-made reverbs. I think there were four of them, starting with one that was fairly small. It had a speaker in it, and a microphone, and they can send your singing through that and get the sound of that box. Then there'd be another one bigger, and then another one way big, and then one really big. They could adjust that sound themselves rather than have a machine do it. They had the best microphone and the best speaker in there. Reverb is better now, but at that time it wasn't technologically advanced.

So when I sang my songs, it would go from me into the box, and then they would record what came out of the box. It was cool. Each box created its own sound. Kind of like if you go in a small

The Muscle Shoals Rhythm Section also known as the Swampers. From left, Roger Hawkins, Barry Beckett, Jimmy Johnson, David Hood.

bathroom, you get one kind of reverb. If you go into a larger bathroom, you get a different reverb sound.

We'd start at the house and have breakfast. I started everyday shooting baskets with Bob Seger. I was much better than Seger. Are you kidding?

In the end, we created the album using the Tower of Power horns – we flew to Los Angeles — and Greg Adams charted everything. Then we flew directly to Miami, Criteria Studios, and put in the Bee Gees strings. We went to New York to shoot the album cover photos. It's got the Memphis Horns on it too. It was first class all the way.

I finally got home to Minneapolis, and I got a call saying they're not going to release the album. Yeah, they're not going to release the album.

So, Richard Perry, the former RCA producer who now had his own label, Planet Records, tried to buy it. And Muscle Shoals tried to buy it back, but RCA said no.

Walter Hofer, a national music attorney, finally told Ron Geslin, "They're going to write this off and they'll triple their money. They're just writing this off. They're not going to go for it." Jimmy Johnson and Barry Beckett and I had become good friends, and they sent me a master. Jimmy said, "I don't know what's going to happen with you or the band, but I'm going to send you a master in case you want to make this into a CD." I said, "Fucking right I do." We've sold thousands of those.

I got to live with Bob Seger for three months. It was an incredible experience, the whole thing helped me musically for the rest of my life.

That was a good album, I wish RCA would have released that album.

HAMMOND B3

I've just got to say something about the Hammond B3 Organ, the greatest instrument that was ever invented. It was all accidental of course. He was trying to build a continuous tone generator. He had the source to program the notes. This guy Hammond made Hammond organs. They're a little antiquated for nowadays, but you could create a lot of sounds with it, but you had to know how to use it. You had to know how to use the volume pedal. It wasn't just a high or low volume, he called it an expression pedal. With your foot, you could make a sound.

For me, it was good. I started playing it in Los Angeles. We were doing some demo tapes with some actor. His name was Aki Aleong. He said I think you guys should record. I can't remember what shitty little organ I had at that time, but we went over to this place on Devonshire where we ended up recording quite a bit. In fact we made our first album there. They had a Hammond. The guy said you should just use a Hammond instead of whatever you're using. It became the big sound of our first album.

Jim Johnson always said that keyboards gave him a headache. Because they always sounded so bad, you know those little Voxes. But the Hammond had a mellower sound. The spinning speaker, called a Leslie, is part of the sound.

The top part of the Leslie speaker has a horn in it, and the horn is balanced on each side so it spins. There's sound coming out one side, fast, and it has a distinct sound of its own. The bottom is a woofer with a rotating baffle.

It was ingenious. I don't know who this guy was, but it was unbelievable. Try to buy one these days. It's ten grand for an organ and a Leslie.

The problem is they're so fucking heavy. What I did is have them chop the legs off, because they had no performance quality to them, and then I went down to Central Avenue, a place called EMI, and I had them enclose it in an anvil case with steel corners. They put the whole thing in that, and then you could turn it up on its side, and it had four wheels. It was easy to roll. Two guys can tip it up, but two guys can't lift it up. We got a little fold-up stand to put it on. It was sturdy enough and it was portable enough. We put that thing on airplanes.

The original Hammond B3 Organ was made from 1955 to 1974. They are now considered collectors' items with an average price of $6,000 to $12,000.

James and daughter, Natalie, at her wedding. (Photo courtesy Jan Rangel)

Chapter Ten

Reborn

And even though we ain't got money,
I'm so in love with you, honey,
And everything will bring a chain of love.
— *Danny's Song*, Kenny Loggins, 1971

James Walsh:

I was still playing in a band. I was still with the Gypsy guys. We played at the Cabooze, one of the major rock venues in the Twin Cities. We had a deal that for $25,000, we would play there five times a year. He didn't want us playing at the Union Bar, and so we made a deal.

So we were playing there one night, and I see this beautiful, beautiful girl in front of me. And I'm doing my usual James Walsh routine. I'm singing to her. She's smiling. So we end up going out after the show. I started seeing her. I found out later that she's 17 years old. I don't know how she got into the Cabooze. I lived out at Georgetown Apartments on the East River Road. She moved in with me and we lived together for eight years.

She decided she wanted to have a baby. So, I said, "Okay we'll have a baby." She gets pregnant. She was another one of my stupid mistakes. She was a trophy, not a person to me. She was like a car. So now she's pregnant and about three weeks into the pregnancy, she sat me down one night and said, "I want to have an abortion."

I said, "Well, you know, Jimmy doesn't do abortions. That's not something I would be a part of." At that point, our relationship took a turn, and I said, "Well, I'll take the baby." She said okay. I had an attorney and we went to court in Minneapolis and she signed all the papers. Two days after she had the baby she left for New York. That day, I went to Unity Hospital, and – at 38 years old – I picked up a baby, baby Natalie. Everything changed. Not some things, but everything. That was my reward.

I took this baby home. I lived in Columbia Heights and I started raising her by myself. My sister and my mom helped, they helped a lot. I knew nothing. I had other children, but I was absent for much of their childhood. We were on the road all the time. I didn't have much interaction with those children, and it was terrible. I've had long conversations about how sorry I was for choosing this career over them. You get caught up in it.

I took her home. I would struggle, and my mom would come over. The first time I put her in the sink to give her a bath, I didn't know how slippery babies can be, and she went under water, and I was fishing her out.

I used to sleep with her under my robe, I would tie the robe around her, and just sleep in my chair.

Two years into doing this I ran out of money. A friend of mine who was an attorney, Gary Clark, was friends with Doug Brown. Doug and he were having lunch and Doug said, "I need somebody to manage my studio downtown." Gary said, "Well there's somebody who needs work, and his name is James Walsh." He told him the story.

I went and interviewed, and ultimately I got that job. Now I had the baby and I had a good job, a great job. I was a studio manager and producer. Then the Metro Records thing came to mind, and he asked me what I thought about that and I said it was a tremendous idea. So we started Metro Records.

I finally had to take my daughter to daycare. I dropped her off at daycare and I was bawling like a baby.

I had made that mother connection. If you feed a kid and change enough diapers, you're mindset is different.

It was the longest three days of my life. I just kept crying. Finally the person running the daycare said, "Jim, you've got to quit calling here. She's okay." I'd call all the time, "Is Natalie okay? Is Natalie okay?" She said, "Jim, we'll call you if anything happens."

So everything since that time has turned to gold. Everything. I had a great job, I was making a $100,000 a year. I was a different person. People who knew me said I'd become a different person. I said, "Well, I've learned some things."

My daughter, who is now 34, and I were very, very close. I'd always tell her, "It's you and I against the world." She has two children, and they are my dear grandchildren.

So everything I've tried to do or aspired to do has turned to gold. I've got enough money to last until I'm 92.

I had a come to a reality moment where my level of responsibility had changed. I was being a mother. I came to realize all the mistakes I had done in the past. All the terrible things I had done to my wife, Pat. It just made me a better person.

STUDIO RECORDING

Over the years, I produced 110 CDs for people. They'd come in and we'd release product. Eventually they gave me a piece of the action. It was a very nice time, and that was when Natalie was young, so it was all good.

I have the ability to take an idea and make it into a song. A lot of people can write a song, but they can't write an arrangement of the song. They can't enhance it. We had a really good crew, we would work at it every day. I would do a lot of the work at home, and I'd come in and pass out the parts, much like we do now when we record my songs. We did it every day. We'd get there at 10, we'd record until 5, and then we'd go across the street to the Monte Carlo, and we'd come back at 6:30 and go until midnight – every day. It was pretty cool. Great engineers, great musicians, Bob Jones, Kenny Wilson, Bill Davis, Chico Perez. We had many great drummers including Michael Bland, who was Prince's drummer. It was very good for me.

Muscle Shoals really helped me. I saw how the best had done it. I saw how quickly they did it. I saw how organized they were. That's the only way that could have worked. I was responsible for $35,000 a month in downtown Minneapolis to make that studio run. I used many, many of their tools. Having a little bit of local success helped me too because a lot of the people had heard of Gypsy. They thought, "This is a good guy." Once I tooled a couple of their songs, they got the idea. They saw that I could see their vision, and I was able to enhance it into a better color.

I have a platinum record with Sheryl Crow. I was the production manager. She had received a call from a movie company regarding one of the songs she had pitched. "Keep on Growing" was the song. It was in the "Boys on the Side" movie. She was appearing at

Jonny Lang was born Jon Gordon Langseth in Fargo in 1981. By the age of 12, he was playing for friends, and not long after he joined a local blues band. He soon became the feature of the band, and it was renamed Kid Jonny Lang and The Big Bang. At a date in Minneapolis at Bunker's, arranged by James Walsh, Lang was signed to a recording contract with A&M Records, then a major label in the United States. Lang was 15 years old. His second album for A&M, Wander This World, received a Grammy nomination. In 2006, a gospel-influenced album, Turn Around, won a Grammy. In his early days, he always performed barefoot, a tribute to blues musician Luther Allison, but several near-accidents with an electrical shock on stage convinced him to wear shoes. He has toured with the Rolling Stones and B.B. King, and he played in Eric Clapton's Crossroads Guitar Festival in 2004.

Diana Pierce, a news woman for KARE-11 in the Twin Cities, was born in 1955 in California. She studied piano and voice as a child and moved to Los Angeles to be part of a Christian touring group. She was first runner up for the Miss California pageant. She studied broadcast journalism at Boston University before working at television stations in Durham, Norfolk and Fresno. She joined KARE in 1983, a job she kept for nearly 33 years. It was during this stint that she decided to use her singing talent to record a Christmas album at Metro Studios. James Walsh is listed in the credits as arranger, keyboardist, producer and background vocalist. Natalie Walsh is listed as a singer in the chorus. Longtime Gypsy band member Bob Jones is listed as a background vocalist. True to her profession, she also lists her hair stylist in the credits. Since her retirement, she has been involved in dozens of volunteer activities.

Northrup Auditorium, and her manager called me and explained the situation. They've accepted this song, but they needed to record it in a hurry. So I cleaned out the studio calendar, and she stayed in Minneapolis. I oversaw the production of this song.

It was horrible working with Sheryl Crow, spending time with her. Hah, it was fantastic. She'd be in my office laying on the couch, driving me nuts. I was very attracted to her. It was fantastic. Her guys were very good musicians. They just stayed in Minneapolis. They had a hotel down on Washington Avenue, so they weren't far away. We got the song done in a timely fashion. It was a good experience. We made it relatively easy for them.

I had a gold record with Kid Jonny Lang. I was the co-founder of Kid Jonny Lang. This father and son came down from Fargo. This kid had sold 4,200 copies of a CD up in the Fargo area. He was a young blues player. There was a little problem with Jonny's parents about the direction and stuff, and I think they eventually got a divorce. I told his father that this kid was extraordinary, and he signed a letter of intent with me to pitch this kid for a little bit.

I called Larry Osterman, who I golfed with all the time and who's a music attorney, and he came to the studio and Jonny did a demo. Then we called Larry Hamby at A&M Records, and sent it to him. He came to town a couple of weeks later, and we showcased the kid at Bunker's. Two weeks later they signed him, and the rest was history.

I did GB Leighton, Down Right Tight, and 110 other local people. It was fun. I did the Rockin' Hollywoods, a lot of big names.

I stayed there for a few years and they gave me a percentage of the studio, 15 percent of ownership. One day, I got a call from a guy named Dave Anderson. You might know him as "Famous Dave." He said, "I'm opening a restaurant chain," and Marsh Edelstein, another friend of mine, said, "Maybe you could help me with the music. I need music for 10 Famous Dave's and we want to create our own music."

He said he wanted to do other people's music, and I told him, "Well, you can do that, but that's dangerous because there's going to be royalties involved with that." I said I can do that and write our own music, but he said no, he wanted it to be authentic. So I did four or five albums for him. I used Down Right Tight, a blues and horn band in town. They had a singer named Big John Dickerson. He was a New Orleans-style singer who was really authentic and good. We did a good job.

We opened the store at Calhoun Square, kind of the flagship of the Famous Dave's, and Dave said, "We want you and the band to play." I said okay. I put the whole deal together. We rehearsed, we were ready to go. We had a two-year contract. But just before we started, I don't know what happened, but he changed his mind. I said, "Well, Dave, I've a contract here. This is a lot of money, this is a lot of peoples' lives." Dave also wanted to shelve all the recording we had done. He had my name on the album, my picture on the albums.

I called Larry Osterbis, an attorney, and told him the story. He made one call to Dave Anderson's attorney, Bill Mauer, and Bill said to come down and see him. So I went down the next day, and I told Bill, "I'm very sorry, I don't know what happened." He had seen the contract, and he said, "Don't feel bad, don't worry about it. I have bailed Dave out before."

I guess I had known that Dave's mother, Marge, was founder of the Grand Casinos in Minnesota and Mississippi, and Dave was filthy rich. Bill said, "What do you think your damages are?" I said, "I have no idea. I was just told to come here." He said, "I'm going to write you a check, and I'm hoping this is enough."

And he wrote me a check for a hundred thousand dollars.

So there I am driving down Central Avenue again, I've got a check for a hundred thousand in my pocket. So I put that in the bank, and I put $25,000 into a trust fund for Natalie's college, which she used wisely.

Sheryl Suzanne Crow was born in Kennett, Missouri, in 1962. She was a majorette and a state track champion in high school, and got her degree at the University of Missouri in music education. She taught grade school and sang in bands and did commercial jingles for clients such as Toyota and McDonald's. She toured with Michael Jackson, and did background vocals for Stevie Wonder and Jimmy Buffet. She hit the charts with "All I Wanna Do." In 1995, a song she had pitched for the soundtrack of the movie "Boys on the Side" which featured all women singers, was picked, and the song was recorded at Metro Studios with James Walsh as the production manager. The song was originally on the Layla album, written by Eric Clapton and Bobby Whitlock. It was released on the flip side of "If it Makes You Happy." Crow has gone on to sell over 50 million albums.

James Walsh at a recording session. At right is Bobby Jones and in the back is Chico Perez.

I did a CD for Diana Pierce. She was an anchor woman for one of the television stations in the Twin Cities. She sold a lot of copies just based on her celebrity.

And then they decided to sell the studio because they were moving GMA to Las Vegas. They got an offer they couldn't refuse from a guy named Robert Pickering, who decided to buy it for his sons. Part of the deal was that I would stay on for two years as a consultant for these two kids.

For many years, the recording studio was James Walsh's place of employment.

James Walsh on keyboards and vocals in the Killer Hayseeds. (Photo courtesy James Walsh)

CHAPTER ELEVEN

WORKING YEARS

On the road again
Like a band of gypsies, we go down the highway
We're the best of friends
Insisting that the world keep turnin' our way
And our way
Is on the road again
I just can't wait to get on the road again
The life I love is makin' music with my friends
And I can't wait to get on the road again
— *On the Road Again*, Willie Nelson, 1980

JAMES WALSH:

Let's see if I can sum it all up. I was five years old when I got a drum, and I was 12 when the summer band bug really got me. I was 13 when I could hear Rick Ballot's band practicing in the basement, and I hopped in the window well to hear them.
1963-64 – The Coronados. I played the accordion at first, then the portable keyboard, and I was a singer.
1965 — Rick Ballot and I took a couple of people from the Coronados, and made a band called the Hot Half Dozen. That turned out to be a better band because we had better musicians. Dick Shapiro got involved with us. Bill Diehl had an agency called the Central Booking Agency. They came out to hear us play, so we signed with them. The big bands were the Underbeats, the Avanties, the Accents and the Chancellors. The Hot Half Dozen was kind of moving up the ladder, starting to play at the same places.
1966 – We played at the Prom Ballroom with the Underbeats. After the show, they said they were doing some recording and they needed a keyboard player. They asked if I would like to do that,

and I said, "Of course I would." Later they asked me to join the band.
1968, November — the Underbeats moved to California.
1969 – 1975, Lived in California, hated every minute of it. The band had run its course, four albums, made a bunch of bad decisions. Nothing happened. I decided to come home.
1975 – Got in trouble dealing drugs, and my attorney told me to cool it for a couple of years.
1976 – I joined a band called Free and Easy. I played with them for several years.
1978 – I wrote a song, "Cuz, It's You, Girl." I sent it to Warren Schatz at RCA records, and he fell in love with the song.
1978-81 — We were the James Walsh Gypsy Band. The second album, the Muscle Shoals album, was not released. So once again we regrouped, but under a different name. Now we were called Jumpstreet and that lasted for about three years.
1980s — We played as Gypsy for a while in the 80s. But at that time we were starting to drag it through the mud, so I bailed on that.
1986 – Natalie changed my life.
1988 — Got the job at the studio and worked there for 10 years.
2002 – Joined the Killer Hayseeds and played with them for eight years.
2010 to the present – Gypsy forever. And Midas Touch at Mancini's.

Along the way, I had some jobs outside of music, usually when I was playing in a band.

I worked at Warners' Stellian for a few years. Jeff Warner was a friend of mine, and he was a big fan of Gypsy. We became very close friends, and we still are today. They were opening a new store in Woodbury, and he said, "Why don't you come out here and open the new store as a salesman?" I worked there for three years, and I was the number one salesman for Warners' Stellian for each of those years. I sold $1.4 million worth of appliances at an average box cost of $647. I was moving a lot of metal and doing well. I wasn't loving it, but I was still playing music in some form at that time.

I was going down the street to Keys Café to eat, which was in the same mall as Warners' Stellian. The manager, Doug Noxheim, came out one day and saw me and said, "Hey, you're James from

Two non-musical stops on James Walsh's journey were at Warners' Stellian appliance store and Keys Cafe, both in Maplewood.

Walsh played piano and sang for the Killer Hayseeds for eight years. (Photo courtesy Jan Rangel)

Gypsy, aren't you?" I said, yeah. So we became good friends and he still comes to every show. "Hey, I'm looking for a restaurant manager." I said, yeah, I'll take that. So I became the assistant to him for a number of years.

I managed Keys Café for 10 years, and it was the largest one they had at that time. There were 63 employees, all working for me.

One night four people came in and sat down at the table. I was watching them, and all four of them were on their phones. And they stayed on their phones. Finally the food came up, and I grabbed it and brought it out. I said, "Hi, I'm James, and I'm the manager. I just wanted to make sure everything is all right. I've just got to know, though, who are you guys talking to on the phone?" They looked at me and said, "Each other." Honest to God, I wanted to bat them off their chairs and beat them up and then eat their food. I went back and sat down and thought, "Well, this is the way it is." That's how they communicated.

I think I was in the Killer Hayseeds at that time. I did that until I was 62.

The Killer Hayseeds were the number-one country band in this whole region. They worked four or five nights a week. They made a lot of money. They approached me about doing some recording at the studio, and I said that I'd like to help them do the recordings. They hadn't done any recording, and I said, "There's a right way to do it and a wrong way." Okay. We picked the best songs. They were a little uneducated with the whole studio thing.

They had three singers, but they weren't three good singers. I said that I'd like to enhance their background vocals with my vocal. So I would keep one or two tracks of what they did, and I'd try to enhance that. Guys would try to sing high, and so they'd have to go into falsetto. I can sing that high in my own voice. It makes it thicker and better with a whole voice. We did the album and I did some keyboards on it to give them a fuller sound. They sold a lot of CDs. They put on the album, "Thanks to James Walsh. We now call him the fifth Seed."

They approached me a few months later about playing keyboard with them live. I said, "Yeah." We had a really good run. It was a lot of work, a lot of driving, but they had a good crew and it was a lot of fun. There were a lot of big venues. We played at WE Fest. We played at a lot of summer festivals. People would come back year after year to hear them.

Ross Florand, Darin Essery, and Todd Ernster were the heart of the band. We called them the partners. The rest of us really weren't involved with the goings on of the band. We just said, "Let the partners figure it out." So the band's going good, everything is fine and Ross has a heart attack. He'd had heart trouble before. He lived in Stacy. They took him from his house in Stacy to Abbott-Northwestern. They did CPR on him all the way. He lived for a couple of days, but his heart was too weak and he died. We had to rethink the band, and we got another bass player. He was really good. But the core of the band had broken up. Jerry Archambault, who now plays in Gypsy, was part of that band.

We got a call one day that Darin, the fiddle player and lead singer, was working as a framer on a house up in Sauk Rapids and he fell 18 feet unto a garage slab. He tried to catch himself, but he

Walsh helped the Killer Hayseeds produce an album. The band called him the "Fifth Seed."

was going too fast and he landed on his head. Luckily, one of the paramedics said, this guy's fucked up but not dead. The medic called and got him helicoptered to North Memorial. It was a long process and to this day he isn't right. I always call him at Christmas. He tried to come back, but he couldn't remember the words. He kept insisting, "I'm coming back, I'm coming back," but that was his inner will. We made the painful decision to let him go. We hired a young girl named Jillian Ray to play fiddle and sing, and we really got the band going good again for a while, but then it broke up.

It was a really good experience for me. It was a different genre of music. I'm a rock and roll guy, and this was country. But I'm adaptable. I think I helped them with my vocals more than my piano playing. I sat down and learned some stupid country licks. We got through it, it was good, it was fun.

You look on this list, and every band I was in, every band was always a good band. I've been very, very lucky that way. And, I'm trying to stay humble, but every band I've ever been in I've made better.

The band I'm in now is called Midas Touch. They were an average band, and now they're much better. But it's an easy gig for me because it's a no brainer. It's not my band, I don't have to worry, there's no trucks, no road crew, no hotel, I just drive over to Mancini's, make a couple of hundred bucks and go home. I play piano.

There's a chemistry in a band. When it all comes together, and the timing is right, it's extraordinary. I've been very fortunate.

Being in a rock and roll band is often not very glamorous. Being on the road is really hard on you. Taking a bus a long distance is hard. But flying is also hard, you've got to be at the airport at a certain time, get up early, this and that. But there's something romantic about it, I'm not sure what it is.

When the people go home, the musicians don't go home. There might be a couple of more hours of taking down that equipment and bringing it home.

Another band I played with was Down Right Tight, a soul and funk band in town. I was with them for a few years.

We put the Gypsy thing back together while I was at Keys. Bobby Jones, Bill Davis, Randy Keeley, Stan Kipper, Chico, it was pretty much the same guys who were in Jump Street. We were kind of a modular band.

The Gypsy band had never really broken up, we were just under another name for a while. I can't tell you when that was, when we got together and went after it again. We played the Myth a lot. We opened for REO Speedwagon at the Myth, and a couple other groups. The Myth Nightclub was in Maplewood. It was poorly run, but a fabulous venue, a perfect music venue.

This current band has been together way longer than the original band. The originals were together from 1969 to 1975. That was it. These guys have been with me the whole way, kind of a different path, but still very successful. They play in other bands.

God sent me Travis Schilling. Bobby Jones was the bass player, and Al Tossel played bass on the album. He plays in Midas Touch which I play in on weekends. Jerry Archambault told me that I needed to hear Travis Schilling. I gave him three songs to learn, and he came in here and fucking killed it. He's a virtuoso bass player and bass teacher. He's a great guy, and he just fit right in. I hope he'll be with me a long time, very dependable. I play with him in church.

I think the legacy of Gypsy is the music, the longevity, and that we were able to make a mark that will last beyond my life. What I should do is shoot myself, and then we'd sell tons of CDs for a while. But then somebody else would get the money.

I think Gypsy was ahead of its time, kind of progressive rock and roll. It has withstood the test of time. It's crazy.

What made the music different was a combination or a chemistry of people. Bands are like football teams. You can have a great team like the Vikings, but they have no chemistry. Maybe a better analogy would be the Twins in those two years where they won the World Series. They were not the best team in Major League baseball, but the chemistry at that time was perfect. It all aligns itself.

Me, Jim, Rico, Doni and Jay had a chemistry that worked. The creative part was Jim and I and Rico just working hard at it. And then we rehearsed hard at it. When that adventure got going, I was 19. I came out of my musical shell at that time a little bit. The more creative I got, with the spectrum of that trio, they realized that I had more to put in, and on the first album, they really gave me a wide pallet of colors. That was part of that first album, there was a lot of organ, a lot of great hook lines I made up. So it was the chemistry.

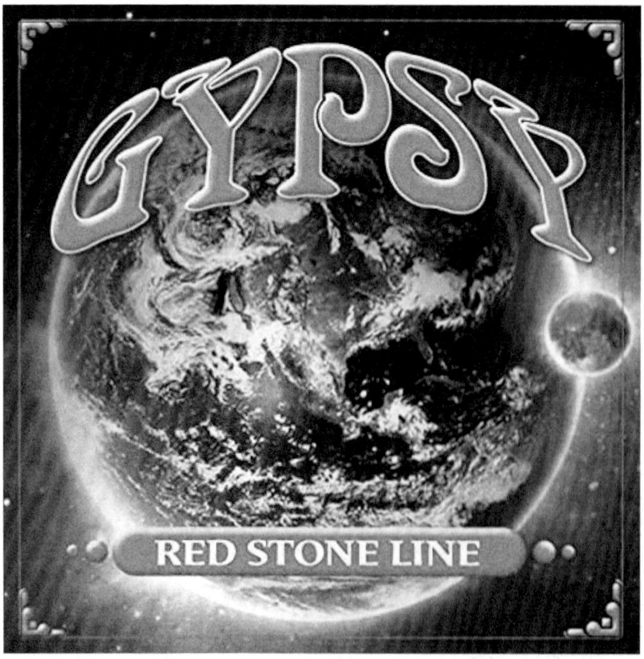

I've had that chemistry since. When Bill Davis, Randy Keeley, and when Bob Jones were in the band there was a good chemistry, and I think we've achieved it again. I really like Bobby Vandell, he's the future.

After nearly succumbing to COVID in 2020, Walsh began writing songs that eventually led to the creation of *Red Stone Line* in 2021. The album has been well received by Gypsy fans.

Jumpstreet was a band that produced an album, *Follow Her Home Tonight*. Walsh stated the band in 1980 and they played throughout the Midwest for nine years. Members of band included: Walsh, Chico Perez, Bobby Jones, Lee Holm, Rob Steinberg, and Brad Swagger. (Photo courtesy James Walsh)

Our last album, *Red Stone Line*, has given us the ability to do something special. This album has gone farther than any album we've ever done. You're getting all the inside stuff now.

It was three writers getting together and sharing ideas. Just like Elton John and Bernie Taupin. They don't do anything together. Bernie writes the lyrics and Elton John writes the music. Not many people know that. The Bee Gees, three geniuses working together. We'll never know how the pie broke down, but you know it was all of them working together. With one writer, there's usually a stream. With three writers there's a stream with some rivers that go out. It was a chemistry.

Progressive rock is rock and roll that transcends traditional rock and roll style. At least for Gypsy, it was rock and roll that had a touch of jazz, a touch of funky music, a touch of rhythm and blues, a touch of country music. It had a touch of jazz fusion.

I'm not sure I can compare Gypsy to any other band. There were a lot of progressive rock bands in the 70s. Frank Zappa. The Doors were a progressive rock band. They had tunnel vision, but their ideas were very progressive.

Running a band is like being a school teacher, or being a football coach. When you're dealing with a lot of personalities, it's important to find a common ground. My common ground is Gypsy, the name and the history and my involvement. I have little or no problem getting people to follow my lead because they want to be involved with the history. And they make more money. Those are all things in my favor.

Everybody's different. So I always draw the line, and I'm always fair. I always share. When we go to St. Louis for two days, those guys will make $3,000 for two days. That's a payoff to me because it qualifies my commitment to them. I share the revenue on the tee-shirts and hats and CDs, whatever merchandise we sell, I share with them.

It's tough, but the minute I find there's a glitch, I immediately deal with it. I don't let it fester in their mind. Because they are musicians, and they do have egos, and they think it's all about me. But it's not. It's all about Gypsy.

I've done that with every band I've ever been in. Now, I don't lead every band I've ever been in, but I always take over the band if that makes sense. What do they call that, a coup d'etat? Rick Ballot had the Coronados, he led that band, then we started the Hot Half Dozen, and then based on careful thinking and talent, I was able to be the leader of that band.

And then I was a member of the Underbeats, and Jim Johnson was the leader of that band. When he went into the service, Rico and I took over running the band.

And then I was in Gypsy, and Jim and I and Rico were in charge, and that was run by a vote.

I joined the Killer Hayseeds, and it took me about four months to have an influence in that band. But it was based on songwriting ability, talent, songwriting ideas, and those people wanting the same things I had achieved. The list goes on and on.

And now with Midas Touch. After one of the Bill Diehl Music Award presentations, Dennis Donovan and I talked about joining the band. So I went out and saw them for a month. I took a pad with me and wrote it all down. So I finally got together with the band and I told them they could be a lot better.

Dennis was the leader of the band, and he was happy with my honesty. After I got done telling them my critiques, and that they sang the wrong parts, they had guys singing parts they had no business trying to sing. I told them they were too fucking loud. And every tempo is the same. I was able to use my background in singing and producing to help, and they were gracious enough to listen.

I don't know. It's not an egotistical thing with me. It's just that I prefer quality over anything else. Say you send a guy out to catch a pass ten times, and he only catches two, he doesn't work, that dog doesn't hunt. That's why I've had so much trouble with drummers over the years. I've gone through drummers, 10-15 drummers over the years, and I always tell them the truth. I say, "You can't play this gig."

Gypsy music is very, very, very intense. It's complicated. It's very complicated. We swing from

For the last several years, James Walsh has joined Dennis Donovan and his band Midas Touch, regulars at Mancini's Char House in St. Paul. From left: Tony Gusetti, Bob Scoggin, Al Tosel, Donovan, Walsh.

rock to jazz to country to fusion to funky. If I say to a drummer, can you play this, and he might be able to play one or two of the songs, but he can't play the rest of the songs, then I say, well, I've got to let you go. I'm sorry.

I own the band. It's an LLC called Gypsy Family Productions. I do everything I do under that moniker. Out in California, we were not an LLC and we were signing deals with record companies, but that was a whole different thing. We didn't individually have any contractual arrangement with the guys. We were all signed to Metromedia, and then we were all signed to RCA.

After I came back in 1975, Jan Rangel, who has legal experience, put our LLC together and she runs the business end for the most part. She does everything, administers checks, takes in the money, takes care of my taxes. She's made it relatively easy for me, because I'm no good with numbers.

We're a business like any other business. It's a constant struggle. In order to go to St. Louis, which we've been doing every year because we have a major following down there, I need to put out about $5,000. That's just for us to physically get there with travel, merchandise, some food expenses. I used to pay for the rooms, but I got smart later in life and I make the venue pay for the rooms. So we usually get 12 rooms comped for three days which is a tremendous expense we don't have to pay.

When I got COVID in 2020, that was kind of a miracle. I was really sick for two weeks, almost go-to-the-hospital sick, but in the back of my mind, I said, "Don't go to the hospital." I stayed home, and Tere took care of me. The next week I started feeling better and I was getting some sleep, and these songs came to me. Two at a time. "Change the World," that was the hook that came into my mind. "Forever Came Yesterday," that was about Stan's wife who passed away. "Screams of a Dying World" was a direct hit to the gut of the United States and this path we're going down. They all came to me two at a time.

Pretty soon, I had four songs, and I don't write anything down. So I called the studio, and I called the guys, and we recorded two and then we recorded four, and everybody said this is good shit. Then six, then eight, then ten, they kept coming to me. We recorded all of January 2021 and part of February. That was the weirdest time for me, because usually I don't write that prolifically. I memorize the words.

We recorded at Winterland Studios in New Hope. The person that owns it is a guy named Todd Fitzgerald, and he used to be a student of mine at Music Tech. I was a teacher there for five years, and he was in my class. I realized he was there for the right reasons. I pulled him out of there after he graduated and he worked at my studio. And now he has a studio of his own. My gut feeling was good. So we've been together for 30 years, and he takes care of me really well.

I'm working on a project right now. These people are coming in from Myrtle Beach, South Carolina. I've written two songs for them. I did some work for them last year, the guy is talented, he's a good singer, but he didn't have any songs of his own. He won best singer and best song of the year and it was my song. So now he wants to come back this year, and I've been penning some songs for him. I just think of them and then I memorize them. It's actually kind of bad, I should write things down. When I did the latest CD, I did write the words down, and part of the chord structure. But generally I just memorize everything.

It's not a problem working with a band. They're the caliber of players I don't have to drag them around by the nose, I can give them as much rope as I want. They'll be very creative in their own way. So I just let the rope out until a voice goes off in my head. That's not right, that's too far. But they're all creative guys.

These songs I'm working on now, I've got them pretty much taken care of. I need another verse or two. Then I'll be there. I'm weird. This has been going on all my life. It's just crazy. Last year when these guys came into the studio, they said, "Oh, this was sick, you make it look so easy." It's just like anything else, though, if you do something long enough. A blind squirrel will find a nut, you know. I've got it down, I can produce, I can create, I can run the studio, everything in the studio is by me. I always meet the engineer a couple of days before we go in, and I explain what we're doing.

I'm really good at what I do. And that's not braggadocio. Is that a word? But I fucking really can make music happen in a studio, all by myself. I've always said that when I was at Muscle Shoals with Jimmy Johnson and Barry Beckett, I didn't sit there like a drunken sailor. I sat and watched. I watched every fucking move they made. The world's greatest players with the world's greatest producers with the world's greatest equipment. I watched every fucking move they made.

I'm hanging in there. I still get a thrill when I play before people. I still get a thrill when friends are there.

Jumpstreet on the back cover of their album *Follow Her Home Tonight*. (Photo courtesy Jan Rangel)

Recording a studio session for a South Carolina band in 2022, James Walsh and Todd Fitzgerald sit at a console at Winterland Studios in New Hope. Fitzgerald, a former student of Walsh's, owns the studio. In the back is Brian Dougherty, the sound engineer for the band, Gary Lowder and Smokin' Hot out of Myrtle Beach. One of the songs recorded in the session went to number one on an East Coast music chart.

INTERLUDE —

IN THE STUDIO

By Al Zdon

The first thing you might notice about people recording a song in a studio is the extraordinary skill of everybody who has gathered for the task. They know what they're doing, and once they get going they don't waste much time.

That doesn't mean there isn't a lot of down time, as is prevalent in the music business, while equipment is being set up, wires are being connected, glitches are being fixed, and ideas are being explored.

But once everything is ready, they move with professional skill that is amazing for an outsider looking in. At the center of this recording session for Gary Lowder from Myrtle Beach, South Carolina, is James Walsh. Walsh had produced a couple of songs for Lowder last year and helped earn him the award of Male Vocalist of the Year in the Carolinas. Lowder was back to create more good music.

In the recording session I sat in on, Walsh had previously written a song "Any Other Love." When I arrived, the bass player Travis Schilling and the guitarist Bill Davis were meeting one on one with Walsh. They seemed to already know the song, and they were refining their parts along with Walsh's piano. Even their first takes sounded good to me, but they went over it several times, changing things here and there until they and Walsh were sure they had a good sound, the one Walsh had in mind. Walsh generally doesn't write down his songs but has them in his head.

Walsh had the experience of working with Barry Beckett and Roger Hawkins and Jimmy Johnson and the rest of the Swampers at Muscle Shoals for three months earlier in his career, and then running his own studio in Minneapolis for over a decade.

Bill Davis on guitar and James Walsh on keyboard work out the main melody track.

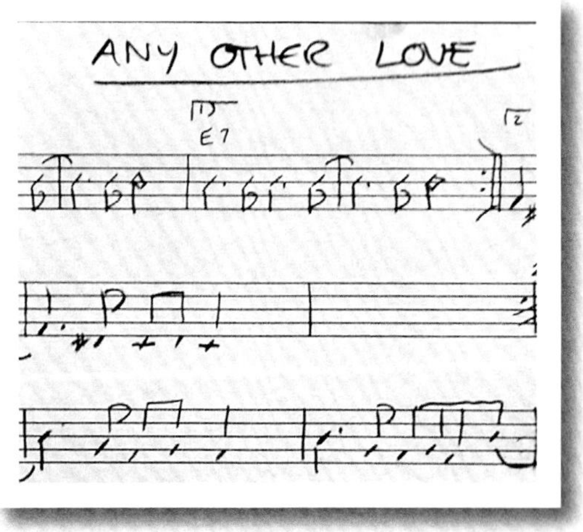

Walsh generally has the song in his head, but a chart was created for “Any Other Love.”

Walsh adds in the background vocals, doing all three harmonies by himself.

Walsh and lead vocalist Gary Lowder, who had never heard the song until the studio session, talk over the recording.

Travis Schilling, Bill Davis and Chico Perez take a break from laying down the tracks.

Jerry Archambault completes the drum track at Winterland Studios.

Also hanging around at this point were the drummer, Jerry Archambault and the percussionist Chico Perez.

My vision of a recording session is the Beatles sitting around a studio and sharing ideas, trying this and that, and ending up with “A Day in the Life.” The reality, at least when it gets down to recording the music, is that the musicians are in separate rooms. Chico had his congas and bongos in one room, Bill Davis had his guitar and amp in another room, and Walsh and Schilling were set up in another room. The only one in the main studio was the drummer, Jerry Archambault. All are wearing headphones so they can hear themselves and each other. Every aspect of the song is recorded on a separate track.

After all the equipment is set up, a tedious process that often involves changing out balky cables and microphones, the musicians simply sat down and played the song. I think it was on the third recording that Walsh thought they had a keeper. I should mention that these are some of the best musicians in the Twin Cities, and they are all members of the current Gypsy band.

Of course that wasn’t the end of it. Some changes needed to be made. In the control room is Todd Fitzgerald, the owner of Winterland Studio, and something of a genius behind the mammoth sound board, the kind you see in the movies with thousands of knobs and other adjustments. Walsh now joined Fitzgerald in the control room as they listened to the basic track of the song. The equipment allows the engineer to replace one track of the song with another.

As Walsh listened to the basic track, first the drummer, and then the guitarist redid their parts.

Davis did what is called a "double," recording the same music over again and then merging the tracks.

Musicians, like every other profession, have their own language, and there were words like "clicky" and "dark" and dozens of others that were perfectly clear to them, but made no sense to me.

With the drums and guitar parts now up to snuff, Walsh went back to one of the cubicles to do the backup vocals. He allowed me in, although I was concerned the clicking of my camera might be picked up by the sensitive microphone.

Now this is the strangest part. Walsh first did the low end version of the backup vocals, and then the next highest part, and then the very highest part where his voice was challenged to hit and maintain the notes. Hearing each one, I thought it sounded terrible. It was sort of like when one of your stereo speakers would go out and you only got one half of the song. Kind of off key. It took him maybe 20 takes to get all the harmonies down, and then it was back to the control room where I got my first chance to hear it all put together. It was extraordinary. It was that lush Gypsy harmony that was always the band's trademark.

One thing the engineer did was to run the tracks through a computer device that automatically adjusted Walsh's voice if he was flat or sharp on a particular take.

There was one more thing to do, Walsh needed to fix up his own piano playing on the main track. This also took 15 or 20 takes with Walsh occasionally stopping and saying, "Okay, I've got it now," a big smile on his face.

And then it was done. It had taken four and a half hours, but the song was basically done. All it needed was the lead vocal, which would be done later in the week when Lowder, who had only heard the song upon arrival that day, had time to learn it. Four and a half hours to make a very tuneful song without a blemish. (And if there is a blemish, it can be fixed.)

Walsh asked me what I thought of the whole process, and I said it was like building a house, brick by brick.

Gary Lowder shuts everything else out as he listens to the final take.

Interview

Bill Davis

By Al Zdon

Bill Davis is a musician's musician.

He's been playing guitar since he was 10 and has been playing professionally since he was 13.

"I was always attracted to the guitar. There was a show on TV called Barn Dance and I would stand in front of the television with my rat tail comb and pretend it was a guitar. I was absolutely fascinated by being a guitarist."

He has had an inside look at the Twin Cities' music scene for almost 60 years, and he was a rhythm and lead guitarist and vocalist for the Gypsy Band through the band's last performance in 2022. James Walsh, the last surviving member of the original Gypsy, always called Davis the band's musical director.

Davis grew up in Columbia Heights and graduated from high school there in 1969. He began playing for a local band, the Dacoyts, when he was in the eighth grade. "We were considered the youngest band in the Twin Cities. We were so popular at one point that we would rent buses to bring kids to where we were playing, and we'd make a little money on the buses."

The band work, especially on weekends, was a detriment to his school attendance. "The vice principal and I used to have talks. He noticed I was missing a lot of Mondays."

He wanted to try college after high school, but with the Vietnam War and the draft hanging over him, he passed. "I thought I'd just play music until I was drafted." Eventually the draft lottery got within three digits of his lottery number, but the call never came.

He has played for the Del Counts, the Hot Half Dozen, and the second iteration of the Underbeats, among many others through the years.

He lists his favorite bands from his career as Gypsy, Transit Authority, Good Friend, Barnaby Rudge, the Renegades and the Underbeats. Barnaby Rudge, a Twins Cities band from the mid-70s, Davis said, was his all-time favorite.

Davis remembers the early days of the rock and roll scene in Minneapolis when he was playing bass for the Hot Half Dozen. "We couldn't get a day off. We'd do stuff like play 28 days in a row — just jump in the truck and go. There were ballrooms, summer fairs, the State Fair and night

Bill Davis cracks a smile during a sound check with Gypsy.

clubs.

"We stayed busy until the band broke up in the spring of 1970. Our last gig was at the Depot with Poco. After watching and listening to Jim Messina play, I knew I had to play guitar again."

In 1972, Davis was playing in a band in Florida. "I got a call from Dennis Libbey wondering if I would like to join a reconstituted version of the Underbeats with Tom Nystrom on drums. I said yes and played with them until March 1974."

From October, 1974, through March, 1975, Davis was back in Florida playing in the house band at the Disney World welcoming center. He returned to Minneapolis to start the band Barnaby Rudge with is friend Steve Johnson.

In 1980, Davis and a friend, Bill Borris, decided to go to California. They had written a bunch of songs together and they wanted to sell them to Los Angeles producers. "We were just writing songs like crazy and some of them were pretty good. Sometimes we'd write a song in 20 minutes, and then do another one."

The two wrote songs for various artists. They stayed six months in California without much success. "We found you don't have to be there in person. Trying to get into people's offices is just about impossible. The mailbox works just as well."

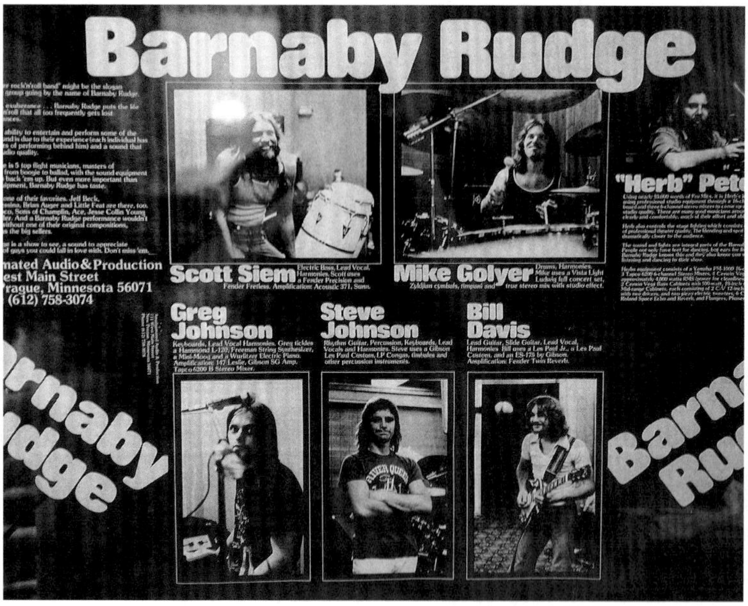

Davis ranks Barnaby Rudge as the favorite band he played with in the early days of Twin City rock and roll.

"One guy told us he couldn't do anything for us — we were too old. I was 30 years old at the time. What we didn't understand was that the industry was moving to indie labels, and that was like a farm system for the major labels. We were trying to interest the big labels."

In 1988, Davis was with the Del Counts, one of Minnesota's longest surviving rock bands. The band consisted of Charles Schoen, Bobby Jones, Brad Swagger, Roger Hunt and Davis, three of

The Del Counts were one of Minnesota's most enduring rock bands. From left: Bob Jones, Bill Davis, Charles Schoen, Roger Hunt, Brad Swagger.

whom would form the nucleus of the new incarnation of Gypsy.

He remembers when Charles Schoen, the founder of the band back in the 60s, stood up after doing one song at the Hopkins Bowl, and said "I can't do this anymore," and walked out. When he returned a few months later, several band members quit and some of them joined with James Walsh to start a new band.

"We wondered what we should call it, but James said, 'Why not call it Gypsy and use that name recognition?' It was an experiment in a way. We didn't know where the waters were going on this."

The first Gypsy booking was at the Channel Inn in Brainerd. Soon they were on the circuit, playing in places like Stillwater and Spirit Lake, Iowa. Gypsy played the Aquatennial, Taste of Minnesota, and at Canterbury Park, where the band would play between races. They also played in St. Louis. The band consisted of Walsh, Davis, Jones, Roger Hunt and Jim Dahl. "We had four natural harmonies in the band, and that was good."

But there was trouble on the horizon. "James and I had our first great divide after we played our last date of 1989 at Westport Playhouse Theatre in St. Louis. We were going to take three or four months off. Three of us – James, Bobby and myself – were scheduled to record on two CD projects.

"After avoiding me for almost a month, James asked me to come in, but he still hadn't told me what was going on."

Davis knew through the grapevine that Walsh had brought in another guitarist to play. He was finally asked to come in to the studio to do some guitar work for someone else.

Meanwhile two technicians from the control room were fussing with an amplifier in the studio while Davis cooled his heels. "I waited for about 45 minutes. I was ready to go, but they couldn't figure out this amp. They wanted a certain sound. Finally I went into the studio and fixed it in about a minute. I'm a guitar player, didn't they think I knew anything about amps?"

Davis did his work, but he was still steaming. As he left the studio, he asked Bobby Jones to leave a message for Walsh. "Tell that fat man to kiss my ass and he'll never see me again."

"I was adamant that I would never work with him again." That was the last communication between Davis and Walsh for eight years.

When Jim Johnson, the leader of Gypsy, returned to the Twin Cities from Los Angeles in 1997 he started a solo career and billed himself as Calvin James. On this album, Johnson's backup musicians included former Gypsy players Doni Larson, Bill Lorden and Stan Kipper.

When Jim Johnson, the founder of the Underbeats and Gypsy, came back to Minneapolis from Los Angeles in 1997, it was Davis who gave him a ride home. "They had dropped him off at B Sharp Music and once we got in the car, we never stopped talking. It was the first time I'd ever met him.

"I saw him almost every day for the next two months. In the time after Gypsy, he had written songs for the Fifth Dimension and Ray Charles. His playing has always had a profound impact on me. He was the ultimate musician."

"When he was going to do his new act, he was going to bill himself as Calvin James, and I asked him why he would want to change his stage name. He said nobody in the Twin Cities would know who Jim Johnson was anymore.

"I said, 'Are you crazy? You know you brought up a whole generation of guitar players. They used to stand in front of the stage and watch every move you made. And I'm one of them.' "

Later, when Johnson won the Bill Diehl Music Award for lifetime achievement in music, Davis saw him at Mancini's on award night. "The place was just packed, wall to wall. I said to him, 'Yeah, nobody will remember you, right?' "

During those years away from Gypsy, Davis was playing in bands like Cowboy Angels and Lip Service, who both were big on the local and regional music scene.

In late 1998, Davis and Walsh had a rapprochement. "We sat across from each other at his office at Oarfin Studios. He apologized to me for what had happened years earlier at the studio. He said we should start a new working relationship, and not let the past stuff get in the way.

"I was blown away."

Davis started working in the studio the next day. "I worked with James, Bobby Jones on bass and Dan Roussin on drums for the next six months – until a water main broke in the main studio. I couldn't afford to be down, so I went back to live playing."

In 2005, Davis was back in Gypsy. "I had heard the band a couple of times. It just wasn't good, it wasn't organized. But I didn't tell anybody. They had five guitarists and they were all playing the same thing."

The band rehearsed, and Davis began working at improving the music. "Jim kind of gave me carte blanche to get the guitars in the proper perspective. I just asked where the rhythm parts were. There should be three parts and they should be complimentary. The other two guitarists, John Domagall on six and twelve string acoustic and Randy Keely on electric lead guitar, bought into establishing three distinct guitar parts for the songs. They were great to work with and enthusiastic to make it sound right. The singing was mainly done by myself and James and Bobby and that was good. We knew where the magic was."

"I think the band sounded good from then on. James said we sounded like Gypsy."

By 2008, the band was doing well, and playing lots of venues. "We opened for ZZ Top and Cheap Trick at Rock Fest in Wisconsin. There were a lot of bus rides, but that was okay because we just got closer as people. You care not only about doing your own job, but seeing how it's complimentary. You couldn't hide your mistakes. We had to play cleanly and play with confidence."
Davis has always had great admiration for Bobby Jones, the bass player for Gypsy. "He's worked about three times longer with James Walsh than any other musician. Bobby has the innate things that James needs. James always said that Bobby could harmonize with a rock. He was very pivotal in providing the main harmony in all those years until he retired."

Over his lifetime, Davis has assembled a small arsenal of guitars. What is left includes three acoustics, including a Martin, and two bass guitars. The electric guitars include two Gibsons, a

A later version of the Del Counts before most of the players became a new iteration of Gypsy. From left: Bill Davis, Bobby Jones, Charles Schoen, Jerry Archambault, James Walsh.

Hagstrom, seven Stratocasters, two Telecasters and a 1959 Les Paul Junior.

Davis has some thoughts on a life in music. "It's been a wonderful career with lots of twists and turns. Unfortunately, I've watched some fellow musicians slowly die that had turned to alcohol and drugs as a coping mechanism. The road travel, plane travel, hotels and motels can eat you up if you don't take care of yourself. When I talk to younger musicians, I tell them to have a good career job to fall back on. The lifestyle doesn't work for everyone."

Davis has a strong opinion on why Gypsy's first album was a critical success and why the later albums never really reached that level. "In hindsight, they should have kept Doni Larson and drummer Jay Epstein. The band chemistry seemed to really work overall. Doni was an excellent bass player, a stay-at-home bass player. Jay had that jazz background. The band seemed to have magic in a bottle.

"The longer tunes really took you on a musical journey, along with the great lyrics and vocals. Don't get me wrong, the replacements – Willie Weeks on bass and Bill Lordan on drums – were terrific additions. Just look at the careers they have had. Unfortunately, it's unexplainable what happened to the next three albums."

Bill Davis got producing credits for this 2015 Gypsy album, "Yesterday - Today - Tommorow," recorded at Winterland Studios. The studiio band was the basic Gypsy Band at that time: Walsh, Davis, Jones, Keeley, Chico Perez, Archambault with horn players Deone Johnson and Dick Jorgenson. The album also includes two orginal Enrico Rosenbaum and Gypsy tracks that had never been released.

A later version of Gypsy, before Bobby Jones retired. From left: Stan Kipper, Archambault, Walsh, Jones, Keeley, John Domagall, Davis.

"In changing musicians, length of tunes, changing record companies… things get altered. It's the old line, 'For every action, there's a reaction.' Anyway, it's just speculation on my part."

As for being considered Gypsy's musical director: "In almost every band, I've been in that role. I'm kind of the musical conscience of the band. What's right is right and what's wrong is wrong. I don't need a lot of external motivation. It's the music. For me, being allowed to play with good musicians is the bottom line. I wouldn't change a thing in my life. Yeah, you have to be half off your rocker to get involved, but I've loved it.

"I will forever cherish the live playing and being able to create music in recording studios with James. We worked so well together. I will miss him."

This interview was done at Bill Davis' home in Anoka over a period of about three months in early 2024.

ESSAY/POEM

BAND OF GYPSIES

By Al Zdon

She was radiantly beautiful, long hair flowing down
Kind of a knowing look as she gazes through the signs of the Zodiac
A jewel-encrusted headband, with shimmering crystal explosions
Confident in her own elegance, she needs no one's approval.

Out of the northern forests they came, their axes in hand
The Grim Leader, the One Who Felt Deeply, the Prodigy.
To the coast they traveled in an enchanted vehicle
To see if their magic would please those in the city of Angels.

They fasted and gave themselves to their craft, day after day
But it was a hard place they had come to, full of hard people.
Their magic wasn't quite ready yet, still evolving
And they remained invisible to those on the watch tower.

And then one day, they found a spot where people gathered
Those people could see that the northern keepers of the light
Could create spells that made all the children smile and laugh
And caused even the ancient ones to break out with dance.

Soon they were performing at a new gathering, and then another
And their fame began to spread across the land of Angels
Great wizards began to pay attention, and sought out the northerners
To offer them a chance to spread their magic across the Kingdom.

The great ones offered the northerners the possibility
Of putting their home brew into a magic ring that all could bring to their homes
But the Gypsy Band knew their creations were now ready
And they were granted the treasure of creating two magic rings.

The Grim Leader brought them to the place of creation
The One Who Felt Deeply summoned up the heavenly words
The Prodigy reached into his soul and conjured up brilliance
And all was captured on the two sacred talismans.

The vision of the warriors was sent out through the land
People from across the Kingdom came to see the northerners
They created several more holy rings while the spell lasted
And then they retreated back to the forest from whence they came.

Their mission was done, they had changed the world.
In time the northerners became just a warm memory of a great era
But across the canyons and fields of the great Kingdom
You can still hear the echoes of their enchanted work.

And the Gypsy Queen still smiles her knowing smile
She knows their deeds were good, and they need no one's approval.

Gypsy played a winter concert in a tent at Crooner's Supper Club in Fridley, Minnesota, in 2023. From left: James Walsh, Bill Davis, Travis Shilling, Bobby Vandell, Randy Keely at a sound check. Jerry Archambault is in back on drums and Chico Perez is on percussion.

INTERLUDE

GYPSY
THE BAND — 2023

By Al Zdon

DENNIS DONOVAN

Dennis Donovan is the manager of the band, helping them get gigs around the Twin Cities. "Yeah, manager, whatever the hell that means." He is also a teacher and lecturer at the University of Minnesota and has developed national programs on citizen politics.

Donovan was instrumental in the recent release of the first two Gypsy albums on CD and vinyl by Sundazed Records. The CD sold out as soon as it was released. Donovan also plays the Midi Cordovox in the band "Midas Touch," a fixture at Mancini's Char House in St. Paul since 1991. It was the first instrument James Walsh played professionally. Walsh also plays in the band. Donovan recalls a time early in his musical career when he was seven and he had to play "My Wild Irish Rose" before 700 nuns.

Donovan also produced the Bill Diehl Music Awards honoring musicians from the Twin Cities classic rock and roll bands. Two of the recipients were Jim Johnson and James Walsh, both of the Underbeats and Gypsy.

CHICO PEREZ

Gypsy's percussionist for many years, he has played in the bands Jump Street, Spirit and the Marauders. A 1966 graduate of Coon Rapids High School, he also grew up on the North Side of Minneapolis.

Playing the congas and other Latin drums, Perez said, "The congas do a figure eight. They play in spots where other people don't play." He played for many years in the Del Counts.

His association with Gypsy goes back to the 70s when he once auditioned for the band. He has been a part of the band for about 20 years. "I go way back. I love this band because the music is original, and I love original. The writing is so good, the incredible vocals, and the drumming is so wonderful."

TRAVIS SCHILLING

Travis Schilling is a native of Alpena, Michigan, where he started playing bass when he was 15 years old. He came to Minneapolis to go to school at McNally Smith College of Music, and then stayed on the staff as a teacher for 13 years.

He has played with Tim Sigler, the Atlantis Quartet, and in church bands. He was the bassist for blues singer Renee Austin.

He knew James Walsh through the years from the Minneapolis music scene and then auditioned for the band when longtime bassist Bobby Jones retired. "I learned 12 or 13 songs in a week for the audition."

"It's special playing with Gypsy, they have an incredible lineage and heritage. When they first came out, maybe the world wasn't ready, but they kicked the door open for everyone else. A lot of the today's music is on their coattails. I'm honored to be a part of it."

JERRY ARCHAMBAULT

Jerry Archambault hails from Faribault, Minnesota, where he is still part of the family business. His interest in drums came from his dad who played in wedding and country bands. Jerry started drumming when he was five or six years old.

He drummed in high school bands including the Revelles, and has since played with Tim Sigler, Eric Church, IV Play, Rockie Lynne, and he plays at two churches.

"I fell in love with Gypsy music the first time I heard it. The musicianship was amazing, and I love the songs. They were way ahead of their time. James Walsh took me under his wing when I was pretty burned out on music, and he's always been like a brother."

RANDY KEELEY

Randy Keeley of Waseca started playing electric guitar when he was 15 years old and it was about that time he was recruited to play his first gig at a Fourth of July event when a band's regular guitarist didn't make it. His connection with James Walsh goes back 50 years to Metro Sound and Lighting where Keeley still is a vice president. He first played with Gypsy 24 years ago, and has been the band's lead guitarist since 2001. "We don't do a lot of rehearsing, but when we do a show it just falls into place. It feels great. It's a brotherhood of players, and I'm just glad to be part of it. There's a history behind the band that makes their music an art form. I hope we're helping keep the music alive."

Keeley knew Jim Johnson, the first lead guitarist and organizer of Gypsy. "He was the greatest guy, very supportive. When he was buried at Fort Snelling, I went up to the grave and told him that I would do my best to keep it going."

BOBBY VANDELL

A native of St. Cloud, Bobby Vandell remembers going to hear an Underbeats concert there in 1965. "I was addicted to live music, and the Underbeats were my favorite Twin City band."

He started playing the drums when he was 12, and has been in bands since he was 13 or 14 years old. Through the years he has played with the TC Jammers, Dr. Mambo's Combo, Lamont Cranston, The Steeles, and the Hoopsnakes and Bobby Vandell's Real Men of Country. He had an acting role in the movie *Purple Haze*.

He has been noted for his singing as much as his drum playing, and joined Gypsy as one of the lead vocalists.

"They wrote their own songs, and they made a unique sound right out of the gate. And they've always had that lush part harmony. I love part singing. And if you listen to their songs, they don't follow the standard form of pop songs, it's more like classical music. They didn't follow the trend. They were part 60s, part drugs and part creativity."

BILL DAVIS

A 1969 graduate of Columbia Heights High School, Bill Davis's love for music goes back to when he was a child. "I was barely able to stand, but I would watch Barn Dance on television. I knew then I wanted to be a guitar player. I would stand in front of the TV with my rat-tail comb, pretending it was a guitar." He played in several local bands, and was the guitarist for the Hot Half Dozen not long after James Walsh quit the band to join the Underbeats. He played with the Del Counts and Jumpstreet and has been doing Gypsy gigs for many years.

The musical director of Gypsy, he has been associated with the band since the 1980s. "Their music is fairly timeless. Just doing Gypsy stuff, I try to be faithful to the original sound. It's an honor to be playing in the original band."

JAMES WALSH

The only original member of Gypsy, Walsh grew up in Northeast Minneapolis and worked his way up from the Coronados to the Hot Half Dozen to the Underbeats, playing keyboards and singing.

He played with Gypsy from the driving to California days until the band broke up in 1975.

He has played in several other bands including Jumpstreet and the Killer Hayseeds. He ran a studio for ten years, producing over 110 albums and earning a Platinum Record. He is in the Minnesota Music Hall of Fame, and has continued with several iterations of Gypsy through the years, managing to preserve the unique sound of Minnesota's first great rock and roll band.

James Walsh, age 16, sings and plays keyboards in the Northeast Minneapolis band The Coronados. (Photo courtesy Jan Rangel)

Chapter Twelve

Looking Back

There are places I'll remember
All my life, though some have changed
Some forever, not for better
Some have gone and some remain

All these places have their moments
With lovers and friends I still can recall
Some are dead and some are living
In my life, I've loved them all

— *In My Life*,
John Lennon, Paul McCartney,
The Beatles, 1965

James Walsh:

I need to say something about the two guys in Gypsy who were the heart of the band and who are no longer with us.

Jim Johnson was from North Minneapolis. He was a tough son of a bitch.

Jim was always the leader. He was one of the best guitar players in town, and everybody loved him. He loved to rehearse and that was always part of our approach. He was a really good guy, came from a tough family, he was the leader of the band, he called the shots, he called the songs. Jim was a good guy and I loved him. When he passed a few years ago, it was really, really a blow to me.

And then there was Rico, a not-so-tough guy from Highland Park.
We had to straighten him out a couple of times. On a couple of occasions, we smacked him. I told him if he got up I was going to hit him again. He kinda got the idea, and after those times, he seemed to mellow out a little bit. It was a better working machine after that.

Enrico Rosenbaum (Photo courtesy Jan Rangel)

After we started touring and got popular, Rico got involved with some drug dealers in Los Angeles who were trading cocaine for songs. For instance, they would give another band we knew who were very, very popular, cocaine, and the band would let him put a song on one of their albums for the royalties, which turned out to be huge. But this wasn't like a gram, this was like a pound of cocaine. The guy with the cocaine would get his money eventually, but he would get it forever because the band was Chicago. Rico got involved with these guys. He was not a drug dealer. He was the last one of us to smoke pot. We started smoking here in Minnesota when we started to do our demos to go out there. Rico wouldn't smoke pot. Finally when we got to California, he started smoking pot.

These drug guys dropped off a bunch of shit at his house. We were living in Laurel Canyon. About five minutes later some other guys came and knocked on the door and stole the shit. And then the other guys who dropped it off came back and said, where's our money? You owe us X amount of dollars. He told them the story, but they didn't believe the story, or, more likely, they were part of the whole ruse.

Jim Johnson was home alone one day, and these guys came and busted down the door and they beat up Jim. I think they took a guitar or something that was Jim or Rico's. Rico finally gave them a car he had, an old antique car, and eventually got them off his back.

We went to New York to play at the Fillmore East, and he met a girl named Tootsie. She was a New York girl, very attractive, very New York. We didn't know she was a heroin addict. Before we knew it, Rico was hooked on heroin.

When Rico's father died, we were out on the road with the Guess Who, and Rico said, "I'm not going home for the funeral." Jim and I said, "Huh?" He said, "I'm not going home for the funeral." So we took him aside and said, "Look, fuck-face, you're going home for the funeral, or we're going to kick your ass right now." We let the Guess Who know, and they let us off the dates for a couple of shows, but they kept us with them. They understood.

That kind of turned the corner for me with him. That was 1974, and it went downhill rather quickly after that. Rico went on with Tootsie. He wanted to do music, but never could get it done.

The tools weren't all there, plus he was a heroin addict.

I came home, got my fat ass in trouble, and had to lay low for a couple of years. Rico went on with his life, whatever life it was. It couldn't have been great. Tootsie was working and they were both junkies. She left him in late 1977. In the meantime, we had rediscovered ourselves with that record "Cuz It's You, Girl," and got a record deal. The record came out and was doing well.

I got a call one day from Ida, his mother. She was very sad, she was crying, and she said that Rico was in trouble. I said, "What do you mean?" And she said, "He's taken all of my money." He had taken it all to stay alive and to stay in L.A. with his habit.

She asked me to come over, so I did. Rico's original girlfriend, who had stayed in touch with him, Julie McCully, was there. Ida said to me, "Why didn't you put Rico's name on the new album?" This was the James Walsh Gypsy Band.

I said, "Well, Ida, I haven't seen Rico since 1975." He had been telling her to send money so we could put this album out. So he spent all of her money. All of it. I suppose she had her Social Security. So I had to tell her that I hadn't seen him, but that he was fucked up. She couldn't believe it, and neither could Julie. But I said that's just the way it is.

So, not long after that, I get a call from Rico. I said, "Hey, what are you doing?" And he said that he was in town. I said, "Good." He said, "can we get together?" I said, "Absolutely." I went over there and he was very nice. He said, "Can we get together on some songs?" I said, "Absolutely." I told him what I was doing. I think he was trying to reach out.

I called him after that at his mother's house, and she said he went back to California.

I said, "Why?" She said, "He needed a haircut." I immediately knew he couldn't find any heroin here and he was going back to where he could get it.

So we never got together. A couple of weeks later, we were in rehearsal, and getting ready to go out on tour, and we were at the warehouse down at Seven Corners. I got a call, and he had killed himself. He left a letter for Julie and that was it.

So that was sad. I loved Rico. He was a good guy. He was arrogant, self-serving, spoiled. But losing him was bad. His death set me back for a while, just like Jim's did.

PEOPLE IN THE BOOK

There are some people who need to be in this book:

Pat Monahan, my first wife. She sacrificed for me, and I let her down. She followed me to California, back and forth, had two children, and I was gone all the time. I wasn't a good husband, and I wasn't a good father. But she was a good wife and mother.

Shelly Jonathon Walsh, whom I was married to. Again, I was not a good husband, and I was not a good father. At the time I had my own child from a girl named Cindy, who was a trophy wife that I egotistically took into my life. Shelly helped me raise Natalie. She was a really, really good girl, and I love them all.

My wife, Tere Patterson. She came into my life ten years ago, and for the first time in my life, I felt that I was with my soulmate, and the person I belonged with all my life. She has mellowed me out, calmed me down. She takes care of me. Tere's been a big transformation in my life.

RECORDING

Recording has changed so much. I stood in line in Los Angeles, I think it was 1969 or maybe 1968, at a convention. I stood in this two-block long line just to see a two-inch tape. The first big tape. This was just to walk by and look at it. It was like a dead president or something.

The next thing I know, we were in the studio using that two-inch tape, but it was only a 16-track recording. So you would only use a part of that tape. And now all of that is obsolete, and everyone uses Pro Tools digital which I don't like. I like the tape better. Digital's a little brittle for me. With analog, you're imprinting something on the tape, and the low end is better and the top end is better. The top end of digital is very brittle, and I'm very careful about that. When I record something I'll always go out to hear it in my car, and then I'll flip stations to hear other songs and compare it.

WAVES

I still don't get it. I still don't get it. It's kind of sad. I probably could have gotten more out of the whole experience had I known better, if I was smarter. I was a kid following the wave. One wave would come, and then the next one would come, and then the next one. I smoked my way through that whole fucking thing, which probably was a mistake. And then we started taking acid.

Every song tells a story. I try to get involved with every story on every song. When I'm singing, the words are most important. I pay as much attention to the words as I do to the sound. I have such a tremendous respect for the music from the 70s. Our first albums especially. That's a piece of music that turns out to be artwork as far as music.

They're re-releasing our first double album. It will be released on Sundazed, it's the largest distributer of vinyl records in the world. The president is a big Gypsy fan, and he's really excited about this. I cut a really good deal with them, and it came out in 2022. That could change everything a little bit. I'm hoping it does. We're getting more gigs next year already, just from the Redstone Line album.

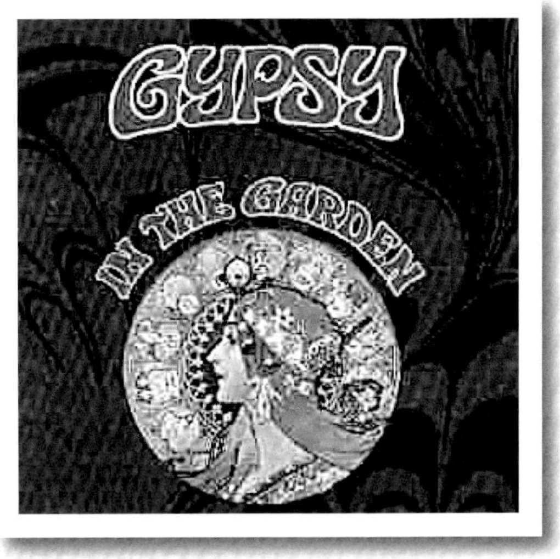

Gypsy's first four albums released in 1970, 1971, 1972 and 1973.

I never came back into town and prostituted myself, or lowered the price, or lowered the bar to make it work. I always said, this band is worth this much, and we won't play for anything less. A lot of musicians lower the price. They say, well we'd rather play than not play. I've never gone by that.

I've always taken a long time making sure the product lives up to expectations.

I've made horrible sacrifices for it, but music is my life, my spirit. I've tried to quit several times, and I've had finale shows, but I can't seem to quit. So now I've made a decision to play until I die. That's how much music means to me. I love letting other musicians experience what I call a real deal kind of a band, instead of just a band. Gypsy has a reputation. Gypsy has longevity. Gypsy has a purpose. Bill and Randy and Chico and Stan have been with me a long time. The other drummer, Jerry and I have been playing together for 27 years. Bobby Vandell and Travis Schilling are the future.

For a musician, you can be a jobber and be in a shitty band, or you find hope and get in a real band. And that's the way I sell it to them. And that's how I make them adhere to the rules. If I have a gig, they're going to be there.

If they have their own band, I have no problem. It used to be hard to maintain the Gypsy sound, but not anymore. Now that I've got this particular group of people together, I don't worry about it anymore.

I have dedicated my life to music. It's a sickness. I've made sacrifices, painful sacrifices, and I was not good to some children. This dream was in my head, and I was chasing that. I was caught up with it. Reality finally set in when I was 38. And then everything turned to gold. It's been that way ever since. I'm the luckiest man in the world.

My visions of grandeur are over. I don't see anything but fulfilling my dream till I die, and that's what I'm going to do. I told the boys I'm not quitting. So I've asked them each to stay with me until I die. They've all made a commitment to do that. It's a great band, great music, great presentation. The young kids don't get it. They want this techno, rap stuff. It's taking over the world and it's crazy. There's guys out there making millions and millions of dollars, I don't even know who they are. They're streaming all that music and making millions. CDs are already almost gone. There's no CD players in the new cars.

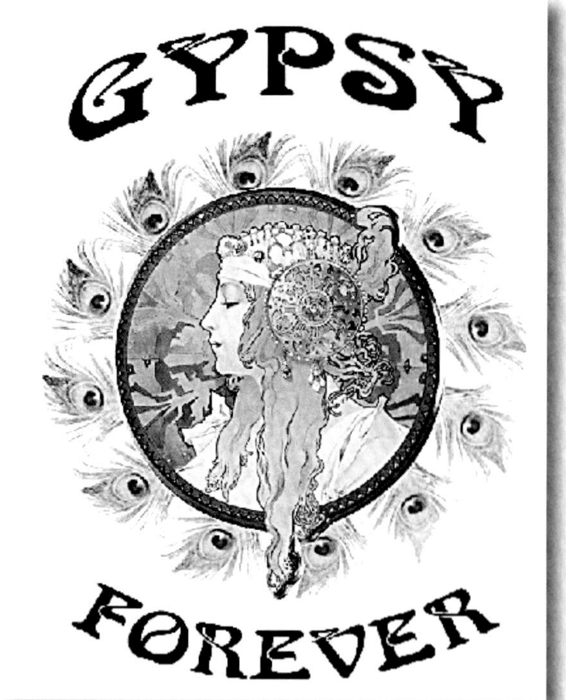

CARS

Speaking of cars, a passion in my life, there have been so many cars that I can't remember them all. They were all my favorites. I have a problem. I get all excited about a car. I'm looking at them all the time. Right now I'm looking for a convertible to buy for Tere for the summer.

I've had a '63 Chevrolet Impala that I invested $1,200 in to get an engine in 1966. Do you know how much $1,200 was in those days? Jack Wheeler was an engine builder in town, and he was considered the best at the time. He put in a 427 Corvette block. He put in dome head pistons. It had all this racing shit all over it. It had four two-barreled carburetors. I took off for school one day, and I'm going down Central Avenue, and the engine goes "Do-do-

In recent years, Gypsy has played at the Wildey Theatre just outside of St. Louis. Thanks to KSHE radio, Gypsy became an acclaimed band in St. Louis and that reputation continues to this day. When the documentary on Gypsy, "Rock and Roll Nomads" was released in 2016 the Wildey stop was billed as the Rock and Roll Nomads Tour. (Photo courtesy Jan Rangel)

do-do-do-do" and quit. The carburetors had sucked all the asbestos off the inside of the hood. It took us two weeks to clear that up.

I've had a new '66 Ford Galaxy 500 that I ordered from Ron Saxon in St. Paul. I had dinner with Ron Saxon and his son Jimmy a couple of years ago. I reminded him that I had ordered a car from him in 1966. I told him it was a Galaxy 500 with a four speed. He said, "I remember that car." It was so rare for a Galaxy to have a four-speed.

I've had two Jaguars, two Corvettes, five Cadillacs, three Mercedes, one XKE, four new Buicks. I had a special order Pontiac. Lee Cotrell who owned White Bear Superstore was a big fan of the band. He said he had this car, it was a special order, a four-speed, with a supercharged engine, so I bought it. Had to have that.

I wish I still had the Jaguars, the XKE, the '63 Chevy. That's 20 cars, and I'm sure there's more. I love cars.

I traded both my Mustangs, a '66 and a '61, for a Mercedes. Plus they gave me five grand. It was a good deal. I'm looking for a Bentley, that's my dream car. A mechanic told me that you're looking at $3-$4 thousand a year just for repairs. Oil changes are $700. I may put that one on the back shelf, for heaven.

Favorite Groups

I loved Steely Dan. I loved the Doobie Brothers when they had Michael McDonald. There's so many I liked and not always for rock and roll reasons. I loved the Boston Pops. I loved the London Philharmonic who have done many concerts with people I like. Sting played with them. I like all kinds of music. I like Garth Brooks, I like the Beatles. I think the Beatles and Garth Brooks had the biggest impact on me. The Beatles took us somewhere we've never been before. Garth Brooks crossed the bridge between country and pop and was on both charts for years. I think he's a genuine good guy. The list could be long. I like Gypsy.

You think about the individual musician on stage, but then there are branches of that that go off to many, many people: Our families, our parents. I gave up too much and I've paid for it ever since. My wife, my children. Next wife, next children. My dream had overcome my ability to think straight.

Doni left before the second album because he had problems with Rico, but also because he had a family back here and they were struggling. We weren't sending any money home. We had a box of rice and a ring of baloney.

I wouldn't have changed a thing, though. I wouldn't have changed a thing. When I got that drum, I knew it. I knew it.

Use of enhancers

I've been drug-free for 15 years. I never was a drinker. I like an occasional vodka gimlet or something. I hate beer.

I went to the doctor one day. I had been golfing, and I went up on the side hill and I felt something snap back here in my leg. I told the doctor I had screwed up my leg. I said I ripped a tendon or something. He looked at me and he said, "Well that's not your problem. Your problem is your blood pressure is 200 and something." At that point I started to be a little more cautious about what I did.

I went to the dentist one time to have my teeth put back in. I was sitting in the chair and the nurse came in, and she took my blood pressure. She dropped the bulb and ran out of the room. Not walked, she ran. The dentist came in and said, "Are you okay?" I said I was fine, and what's the matter? He said, "Well, your blood pressure is 250 over 125. I wouldn't touch you with a 10-foot pole right now."

That's when I started to get my brain better. I've slipped a couple of times on the bus, but that was a long time ago. I don't smoke anymore. And the doctor told me I can't do cocaine anymore because any little amount could blow you out. We used to do mountains of cocaine.

Some of the guys in the band still smoke before we play, but I could never do that.

From circa 1972, Gypsy posed for a publicity picture. From left: Randy Cates on bass, Rico Rosenbaum on guitar, Jim Walsh on keyboards, Bill Lordan on drums and Jim Johnson on lead guitar.

If I was to come over to your house, and I knew we were going to be there for a while, I might smoke. But I get too distracted.

SONGS

You either have a hit song, or songs, or you don't. It's that simple. It's very easy for Blake Shelton to get another hit song. He can just call, and they say, oh, Blake Shelton, don't worry. I've got 20 writers with 20 songs, and he goes through them and picks one. It's the same with Michael Jackson. He didn't write Thriller. He didn't write most of those songs. There's some rich guy who wrote those songs. Achy Breaky Heart was presented 13 times until Billy Ray Cyrus got somebody to see his vision on that song. Now it's a standard.

In the Killer Hayseeds, we were getting really close to getting a deal. I kept telling them, we don't have the songs yet. You just can't present shit. You've got to have some good songs. It separates you from everybody else. It's very, very hard to do. The artists who write well have their own material. The good writers have material they're selling to the good artists, but little Jimmy Walsh from Northeast Minneapolis has to write his own music. I was writing music when I was 15 years old. It wasn't any good, but I was writing music. Stuff just came into my head.

Do you know that music never leaves my head? I have to concentrate really hard to sleep at night, especially if I have a song idea in my head. I really can't lay down when I have a song in my head. I wish somebody would hit me on the head with a ball-peen hammer so I could get some sleep. I stayed up until almost 5 a.m. the other night, I had a song idea in my head and I couldn't let it go. If it isn't in my head, I don't have it.

The words always come first. The hook. You've got to have the hook. "Cuz It's You, Girl," or "Somewhere over the rainbow…" You've got to have the hook. It's like a painter who paints 50 pictures and only sells one of them. They're all skillfully done, but only one is good. And a painter or a musician always thinks his last painting is best. It tricks them in their mind.

I might have a song in my head when I'm on my way home, but when I get up in the morning, it's gone. If I sit down and play it right away, then it gets embedded and I've got it.

Playing with Gypsy is everything that I live for. It's everything that I have left to do. It's all that I've sacrificed for. It's the greatest hour and a half in my life – again. Every job is glorious to me. Every job is emotional to me. Every job is what I've given my life for. Every job is what I've planned, not believing that it could be this way. It's sensational. It's the best feeling of my life. It's my greatest accomplishment.

But to get that accomplishment, you have to sacrifice all these things. I sacrificed my education, I sacrificed my wives, my children, a lot of friendships. But whatever these guys bring at a concert is the greatest accomplishment of my life. You might be an athlete, and you might make your ultimate goal, or make the playoffs, but eventually the clock runs out. But fortunately for me, I can still do this after all these years. Whatever I felt then at Bel Rae Ballroom in 1966, I'll feel again tomorrow night at a concert, but on a larger scale. It has a lot to do with our friends, with our fans, I have a responsibility for these people that have hung on to this all this time. I have a responsibility to do a great show, to do my best, and honor the name.

I don't care how many times the phone rings, I don't care how many problems there are, I don't care how much money I lose – it's kind of sick.

EPILOGUE

The last chapter of this book was completed on March 3, 2023. James Walsh died the next day. He never saw the final book.

My friend, Jim, was one of the last remaining links back to a golden era, a time when a kid could take a break from football at Cavell Park or basketball in the backyard court and join a rock and roll band. At age 13, that's just what he did.

And 60 years later, he would still get up behind that Hammond B3 and create wonderful, sometimes glorious, rock and roll music. He was one of the great singers to come out of the Twin Cities in those days, and he was a great keyboard player, song writer, band leader and record producer until the day he died. He truly was a working musician.

I can't fathom the thought that I'll never hear Gypsy again. They were the premier rock and roll band to come out of Minnesota in that era. I probably saw eight of their last ten concerts. It's hard to imagine never hearing Jim sing "Blind Man" again.

More to the point, his departure to rock and roll heaven leaves a hole in so many hearts. He was far from perfect – which one of us is? – but in the end, you come to realize that he truly had a heart of gold. He wanted to make people's dreams come true, and he so often did.

James' friend and Gypsy's manager Dennis Donovan told me that when James was dying, Dennis left the hospital room so that only family remained. A member of the family came out and asked Dennis to quickly come back into the room. Dennis leaned over James to get his last message:

"Tell the guys I love them."

INDEX